Mohit Sharma
Gurmej Singh Dhaliwal

# A Comprehensive Study of Physical, Physiological and Anthropometric Characteristics of Punjab and Haryana Boxers

**CANADIAN**
Academic Publishing

**2015**

# A Comprehensive Study of Physical, Physiological and Anthropometric Characteristics of Punjab and Haryana Boxers

**Mohit Sharma**
Asst. Professor
Dept. of Physical Education and sports
D.A.V College, Jalandhar, Punjab


**Gurmej Singh Dhaliwal**
Associate Professor & Head,
Dept. of Physical Education and Sports,
N.I.T Jalandhar Punjab

**CANADIAN**
Academic Publishing

**2015**

Price : $27.86

First Edition : May, 2015

ISBN : 978-1-926488-28-8

ISBN Allotment Agency : Library and Archives Canada (Govt. of Canada)

Published & Printed by
Canadian Academic Publishing
81, Woodlot Crescent,
Etobicoke,
Toronto, Ontario, Canada.
Postal Code- M9W 6T3
Phone- +1 (647) 633 9712
http://www.canadapublish.com

# CONTENTS

| Sr. No. | Topic | Page No. |
|---------|-------|----------|
| | Abstract | i – iv |
| 1. | Introduction and Background | 1 – 11 |
| 2. | Review of Related Literature | 12 – 45 |
| 3. | Research Design and Methodology | 46 – 57 |
| 4. | Data Analysis and Research Findings | 58 – 87 |
| 5. | Summary, Findings, Conclusion and Recommendations | 88 – 97 |
| | Bibliography | |

# ABSTRACT

The purpose of the present study to comparison Physical, Physiological and Anthropometric characteristics of Punjab and Haryana Boxers. The subject were selected one hundred sixty (N=160) between the age group of 19-28 years. The subjects were selected purposively random sampling assigned into two groups: Group-A: Punjab Boxers ($N_1$=80) and Group-B: Haryana Boxers ($N_2$=80). Selected Physical characteristics (Speed, Ggility, Balance, Coordination, Reaction time, Power), Physiological characteristics (Vital capacity, Resting Pulse Rate, Peak Flow Rate), Anthropometric characteristics (Standing height, Body weight, Leg length, Upper leg length, Lower leg length, Arm length, Upper arm length, Lower arm length, Hip width, Shoulder width, Chest width, Calf girth, Thigh girth, Chest girth, Upper arm girth, Lower arm girth. The statistical package for the social sciences (spss) version 14.0 was used for all analyses. The differences in the mean of each group for selected variable were tested for the significance of difference by t-test. In all the analyses, the 5% critical level (p<0.05) was considered to indicate statistical significance. The Mean and SD values of Punjab boxers on the sub-variable Speed as 8.02 and 0.53 respectively. However, Haryana boxers had Mean and SD values as 7.87 and 0.27 respectively. The Mean Difference and Standard Error Difference of Mean were 0.15 and 0.06 respectively. The 't'-value 2.289 as shown in the table above was found statistically significant (P<.05). it has been observed that Haryana boxers have demonstrated better Speed than the Punjab boxers. The Mean and SD values of Punjab boxers on the sub-variable Agility as 14.08 and 0.37 respectively. However, Haryana boxers had Mean and SD values as 14.00 and 0.18 respectively. The Mean Difference and Standard Error Difference of Mean were 0.07 and 0.04 respectively. The 't'-value 1.712 as shown in the table above was found statistically insignificant (P>.05). it has been observed that Haryana boxers have demonstrated better Agility than the Punjab boxers. The Mean and SD values of Punjab boxers on the sub-variable Balance as 26.70 and 6.03 respectively. However, Haryana boxers had Mean and SD values as 29.00 and 7.06 respectively. The Mean Difference and Standard Error Difference of Mean were 2.30 and 1.03 respectively. The 't'-value 2.214 as shown in the table above was found statistically significant (P<.05)., it has been observed that Haryana boxers have demonstrated better Balance than the Punjab boxers. The Mean and SD values of Punjab boxers on the sub-variable Coordination as 29.70 and 5.45 respectively. However, Haryana boxers had Mean and SD values as 29.12 and 6.06 respectively. The Mean Difference and Standard Error Difference of Mean were 0.57 and 0.91 respectively. The 't'-value 0.630 as shown in the table above was found statistically insignificant (P>.05). it has been observed that Haryana boxers have demonstrated better Coordination than the Punjab boxers. The Mean and SD values of Punjab boxers on the sub-variable Reaction Time as 0.22 and 0.01 respectively. However, Haryana boxers had Mean and SD values as 0.23 and 0.01 respectively. The Mean Difference and Standard Error Difference of Mean were 0.002 and 0.001 respectively. The 't'-value 1.227 as shown in the table above was found statistically insignificant (P>.05). it has been observed that Punjab boxers have demonstrated better Reaction Time than the Haryana boxers. The Mean and SD values of Punjab boxers on the sub-variable Power as 1.45 and 0.20 respectively. However, Haryana boxers had Mean and SD values as 1.31 and 0.13 respectively. The Mean Difference and Standard Error Difference of Mean were 0.14 and

0.027 respectively. The 't'-value 5.073 as shown in the table above was found statistically significant (P<.05). it has been observed that Punjab boxers have demonstrated better Power than the Haryana boxers. The Mean and SD values of Punjab boxers on the sub-variable Vital Capacity as 3.57 and 0.34 respectively. However, Haryana boxers had Mean and SD values as 3.69 and 0.32 respectively. The Mean Difference and Standard Error Difference of Mean were 0.11 and 0.053 respectively. The 't'-value 2.116 as shown in the table above was found statistically significant (P<.05). But while comparing the mean values of both the groups, it has been observed that Haryana boxers have demonstrated better Vital Capacity than the Punjab boxers. The Mean and SD values of Punjab boxers on the sub-variable Resting Pulse Rate as 76.91 and 3.16 respectively. However, Haryana boxers had Mean and SD values as 74.32 and 2.84 respectively. The Mean Difference and Standard Error Difference of Mean were 2.58 and 0.47 respectively. The 't'-value 5.440 as shown in the table above was found statistically significant (P<.05). it has been observed that Haryana boxers have demonstrated better Resting Pulse Rate than the Punjab boxers. The Mean and SD values of Punjab boxers on the sub-variable Peak Flow Rate as 363.66 and 94.84 respectively. However, Haryana boxers had Mean and SD values as 396.23 and 75.86 respectively. The Mean Difference and Standard Error Difference of Mean were 32.57 and 13.57 respectively. The 't'-value 2.399 as shown in the table above was found statistically significant (P<.05). it has been observed that Haryana boxers have demonstrated better Peak Flow Rate than the Punjab boxers. The Mean and SD values of Punjab boxers on the sub-variable Standing Height as 174.65 and 4.76 respectively. However, Haryana boxers had Mean and SD values as 172.67 and 5.66 respectively. The Mean Difference and Standard Error Difference of Mean were 1.97 and 0.82 respectively. The 't'-value 2.385 as shown in the table above was found statistically significant (P<.05). it has been observed that Punjab boxers have demonstrated better Standing Height than the Haryana boxers. The Mean and SD values of Punjab boxers on the sub-variable Body Weight as 71.65 and 3.10 respectively. However, Haryana boxers had Mean and SD values as 70.15 and 5.15 respectively. The Mean Difference and Standard Error Difference of Mean were 1.50 and 0.67 respectively. The 't'-value 2.230 as shown in the table above was found statistically significant (P<.05). it has been observed that Haryana boxers have demonstrated better Body Weight than the Punjab boxers. The Mean and SD values of Punjab boxers on the sub-variable Leg Length as 101.30 and 3.98 respectively. However, Haryana boxers had Mean and SD values as 100.30 and 5.07 respectively. The Mean Difference and Standard Error Difference of Mean were 1.00 and 0.72 respectively. The 't'-value 1.395 as shown in the table above was found statistically insignificant (P>.05). it has been observed that Punjab boxers have demonstrated better Leg Length than the Haryana boxers. The Mean and SD values of Punjab boxers on the sub-variable Upper Leg Length as 50.76 and 2.22 respectively. However, Haryana boxers had Mean and SD values as 50.15 and 2.20 respectively. The Mean Difference and Standard Error Difference of Mean were 0.61 and 0.35 respectively. The 't'-value 1.768 as shown in the table above was found statistically insignificant (P>.05). it has been observed that Punjab boxers have demonstrated better Upper Leg Length than the Haryana boxers. The Mean and SD values of Punjab boxers on the sub-variable Lower Leg Length as 50.55 and 1.98 respectively. However, Haryana boxers had Mean and SD values as 49.15 and 2.60 respectively. The Mean Difference and Standard Error Difference of Mean were 1.40 and 0.36 respectively. The 't'-value 3.837 as shown in the table above was found statistically significant (P<.05). it has been observed that Punjab boxers have demonstrated better Lower Leg Length than the Haryana boxers. The Mean and SD values of Punjab boxers on the sub-variable Arm Length as 82.15 and 2.33 respectively. However, Haryana boxers had Mean and SD values as 80.76 and 3.20 respectively. The Mean Difference and Standard Error Difference of Mean were 1.38 and 0.44 respectively. The't'-value 3.127 as shown in the table above was found statistically significant (P<.05). it has been observed that Punjab boxers have demonstrated better Arm Length than the Haryana boxers. The Mean and SD values of Punjab boxers on the sub-variable Upper Arm Length as 36.14 and 1.26 respectively. However, Haryana boxers had Mean and SD values as 35.66 and 1.66 respectively. The Mean Difference and Standard Error Difference of Mean were 0.48 and 0.23 respectively. The't'-value 2.054 as shown in the table above was found statistically significant (P<.05). it has been observed that Punjab boxers have demonstrated better Upper Arm Length than the Haryana boxers. The Mean and SD values of Punjab boxers on the sub-variable Lower Arm Length as 46.59 and 2.93 respectively. However, Haryana boxers had Mean and SD values as 44.92 and 1.70 respectively. The Mean Difference and Standard Error Difference of Mean were 1.66 and 0.37 respectively. The't'-value 4.398 as shown in the table above was found statistically significant (P<.05). it has been observed that Punjab boxers have demonstrated better Lower Arm Length than the Haryana boxers. The Mean and SD values of Punjab boxers on the sub-variable Hip Width as 30.95 and 2.56 respectively. However, Haryana boxers had Mean and SD values as 31.00 and 2.16 respectively. The Mean Difference and Standard Error Difference of Mean were 0.050 and 0.37 respectively. The't'-value 0.133 as shown in the table above was found statistically insignificant (P>.05). it has been observed that Haryana boxers have demonstrated better Hip Width than the Punjab boxers. The Mean and SD values of Punjab boxers on the sub-variable Shoulder Width as 35.45 and 1.89 respectively. However, Haryana boxers had Mean and SD values as 34.96 and 1.34 respectively. The Mean Difference and Standard Error Difference of Mean were 0.48 and 0.25 respectively. The't'-value 1.881 as shown in the table above was found statistically insignificant (P>.05). it has been observed that Punjab boxers have demonstrated better Shoulder Width than the Haryana boxers. The Mean and SD values of Punjab boxers on the sub-variable Chest Width as 31.05 and 1.90 respectively. However, Haryana boxers had Mean and SD values as 30.22 and 2.03 respectively. The Mean Difference and Standard Error Difference of Mean were 0.82 and 0.31 respectively. The't'-value 2.650 as shown in the table above was found statistically insignificant (P>.05). it has been observed that Punjab boxers have demonstrated better Chest Width than the Haryana boxers. The Mean and SD values of Punjab boxers on the sub-variable Calf Girth as 38.71 and 1.76 respectively. However, Haryana boxers had Mean and SD values as 32.54 and 1.86 respectively. The Mean Difference and Standard Error Difference of Mean were 6.17 and 0.28 respectively. The't'-value 21.49 as shown in the table above was found statistically significant (P<.05). it has been observed that Punjab boxers have demonstrated better Calf Girth than the Haryana boxers. The Mean and SD values of Punjab boxers on the sub-variable Thigh Girth as 55.58 and 1.99 respectively. However, Haryana boxers had Mean and SD values as 51.51 and 2.73 respectively. The Mean Difference and Standard Error Difference of Mean were 4.07 and 0.37 respectively. The't'-value 10.771 as shown in the table above was found statistically significant (P<.05). it has been observed that Punjab boxers have demonstrated better Thigh

Girth than the Haryana boxers. The Mean and SD values of Punjab boxers on the sub-variable Chest Girth as 90.40 and 3.04 respectively. However, Haryana boxers had Mean and SD values as 88.95 and 4.16 respectively. The Mean Difference and Standard Error Difference of Mean were 1.45 and 0.57 respectively. The 't'-value 2.513 as shown in the table above was found statistically significant (P<.05). it has been observed that Punjab boxers have demonstrated better Chest Girth than the Haryana boxers. The Mean and SD values of Punjab boxers on the sub-variable Upper Arm Girth as 29.32 and 2.13 respectively. However, Haryana boxers had Mean and SD values as 25.92 and 1.13 respectively. The Mean Difference and Standard Error Difference of Mean were 3.39 and 0.27 respectively. The 't'-value 12.550 as shown in the table above was found statistically significant (P<.05). it has been observed that Punjab boxers have demonstrated better Upper Arm Girth than the Haryana boxers. The Mean and SD values of Punjab boxers on the sub-variable Lower Arm Girth as 25.86 and 1.20 respectively. However, Haryana boxers had Mean and SD values as 25.04 and 120 respectively. The Mean Difference and Standard Error Difference of Mean were 0.81 and 0.19 respectively. The 't'-value 4.286 as shown in the table above was found statistically significant (P<.05). it has been observed that Punjab boxers have demonstrated better Lower Arm Girth than the Haryana boxers.

# Chapter - I

## Introduction and Background

## Introduction

*This section gives a brief overview and provides a context for the study. This chapter introduces the research questions and provides a review of the literature concerning physical, physiological and anthropometric characteristics of Punjab and Haryana boxers. The chapter is organized in sections covering:*

  i.    *Statement of the problem*

  ii.   *Objectives of the study*

  iii.  *Hypotheses of the study*

  iv.   *Delimitations of the study*

  v.    *Limitations of the study*

  vi.   *Definition & explanation of the terms*

  vii.  *Significance of the study*

# BACKGROUND OF THE STUDY

Sports, games and physical fitness have been a vital component of our civilization, as is evident from the existence of the highly evolved system of yoga and a vast range of highly developed indigenous games, including martial arts. The intrinsic linkage between sports and games and the human quest for excellence was recognized ever since the inception of human civilization, reaching its epitome in the ancient Greek civilization, which was the progenitor of the Olympic movement. As stated in the Olympic Charter, Olympism is a

*"Philosophy of life, exalting and combining*
*in a balanced whole the qualities of body, will and mind".*

So also is yoga based on the complete control of body and mind. Blending sport with culture and education, Olympism seeks to create a way of life based on the joy of effort, the educational value of good example and respect for universal fundamental ethical practices. Olympism recognizes the practice of sport as a human right, to which every individual must have access without discrimination of any kind.

In modern times, there has been increasing recognition of the role of Sports in Development. The International Charter of Physical Education and Sport, UNESCO, 1978 states that

*"Every human being has a fundamental right of access to physical education and sport, which are essential for the full development of his personality. The freedom to develop physical, intellectual and moral powers through physical education and sport must be guaranteed both within the educational system and in other aspects of social life."*

Sports and Games as a vital component of social and cultural life are embedded in the Indian heritage, and can be found in the archaeological excavations of Mohenjodaro and Harappa, the Vedic literature, the Ramayana and the Mahabharata, the Puranas, the literary works of Kautilya, Kalidasa, Panini and Dandin, as well as in Buddhist and Jain literature. They had been seen as an intrinsic component of education and development of the human personality in the philosophical texts of ancient Greece, the progenitor of the Olympic movement. Every civilization has evolved and developed its own indigenous modes of physical endeavour and healthy social interaction through a variety of games and sports forms and events. Apart from being a means of physical exercise and fitness, sports and games have been a medium of entertainment, the generation of a spirit of healthy competition, bonding and pride in the community, and an avenue of constructive preoccupation for active young people.

Sport and physical education have been found to bring individuals and communities together, highlighting commonalities and bridging cultural and ethnic divides. Sport and physical education provide a forum to learn skills such as discipline and leadership, and they convey core principles that are important in a democracy, such as tolerance, solidarity, cooperation and respect. Access to and participation in sport and physical education provide an opportunity to experience social and moral inclusion for individuals and populations otherwise marginalized by social, ethnic, cultural or religious barriers. Through sport and physical education, individuals can experience equality, freedom and a dignifying means for empowerment particularly for girls and women, for people with a disability, for those living in conflict areas and for people recovering from trauma.

The positive benefits of sport provide opportunities for personal development physically, emotionally, socially, and culturally. A number of psychologists have presented studies linking the positive influence of unstructured play on child development, emphasizing that a child's spontaneous self-generated play has great potential to enhance brain development and increase a child's intelligence and academic ability. Sport and play also play an essential role in promoting individual development of women and girls, those living with disabilities and in trauma rehabilitation and reintegration of individuals.

In terms of the competitive aspects of sports also, there has, over the years, been a sea change, in terms of the manner in which they are played, practiced and perceived at the national and international levels. The standards and levels of endurance, fitness and performance displayed by sportspersons have improved exponentially, the number of competitive sports disciplines has increased with the inclusion of many games indigenous to various regions of the world and, with the massive growth and sophistication in the spheres of media and communications, the visibility of competitive sports has grown enormously. In tandem with these trends, there has been increasing emphasis on the creation of high quality infrastructure and employment of sophisticated technology in the conduct of sports events, with a great deal of attention being given to the development of advanced scientific and technical support systems for sportspersons. With all this, sports as an area of activity, has acquired vast new dimensions, with multi-faceted implications of an economic nature and business potential also. Increasingly, hosting of international events is also seen by countries and cities as a means of positioning and show casing themselves in the international arena as tourism, business and investment destinations; significantly, many countries/cities are using these events as an opportunity to revitalize the poorer areas of the cities. The phenomenal growth of satellite television has not only brought international sports events into the bedrooms of billion of viewers across the world, but in the process opened the doors for huge revenue generation through sale of broadcasting rights, advertising, etc. Equally importantly, these developments have a significant impact on the perceptions and expressions of national aspirations and pride, mass participation, and bringing communities together.

When it comes to professional excellence at the level of individual sportspersons, it is observed that the consistently rising level of performance in various disciplines is not only related to basic training and grooming at the early stages (which, of course is of vital importance), but is also a product of a complex interaction of scientific back-up comprising, physiological, biomechanical, nutritional and psychological elements, use of state of the art equipments/accessories, adoption of research based modern techniques and a well planned and strict regimen and schedule. During the past two decades several countries, such as Australia and China, have committed substantial financial and human resources to identifying and developing their sporting talent, which is reflected in the exponential growth in their medal tallies in the Olympics and other mega international events. In short, in today's world, an international medal-winner is not just found, or born, but is created through a well-researched, discipline-specific, scientific processes and education, backed up by appropriate incentives. What also emerges from this is that achieving excellence is not something that can come about as a subsidiary activity, but is a full time occupation. This, in turn, has a range of implications in terms of the need for incentives and career options, etc., for talented sportspersons.

Boxing is an intermittent sport characterized by short duration, high intensity bursts of activity. It requires significant anaerobic fitness, and operates within a well-developed aerobic system. Boxing is estimated to be 70-80% anaerobic and 20-30% aerobic (Ghosh et al., 1995). Boxing's work and rest ratio is approximately 3:1. The rule of the amateur boxing has been changed from $3 \times 3$ round to $2 \times 5$ round in 1990 world championship competition, and then 4 x 2 rounds with one minute of rest pause in between each bout. The nature of boxing requires athletes to sustain power at a high percentage of maximal oxygen uptakes (VO2max) (often above lactate threshold, producing high levels of blood lactate leading to premature fatigue). The primary aim of conditioning for boxing is to delay the onset of fatigue by increasing tolerance of lactic acid build-up, increasing the ATP and CP, to improve efficiency of oxygen use, and to improve recovery between intense bursts of activity (Guidettiet al., 2002).

Few studies have been reported in the literature about the cardiovascular and metabolic demands of boxing (Khanna et al., 1992, 1995 Ghosh et al., 1995). Previous studies on Indian boxers concentrated mainly on body composition, muscle strength, aerobic capacity, and anaerobic power of Indian Boxers (Ghosh et al., 1995; Khanna et al 1992, 1995; Singh et al., 2003). Few investigations into the biochemical parameters of Indian boxers (Garg et al 1985) have been conducted. Therefore, the present work focused on physical, physiological and anthropometric characteristics among Punjab and Haryana boxers.

## STATEMENT OF THE PROBLEM

The problem is stated as "A COMPREHENSIVE STUDY OF PHYSICAL, PHYSIOLOGICAL AND ANTHROPOMETRIC CHARACTERISTICS OF PUNJAB AND HARYANA BOXERS".

## OBJECTIVES OF THE STUDY

1. To find out the significant difference of Physical Fitness Components (i.e., Speed, Agility, Balance, Coordination, Reaction Time and Power) among Punjab and Haryana boxers.

2. To find out the significant difference of Physiological Characteristics (i.e., Vital Capacity, Pulse Rate and Peak Flow Rate) among Punjab and Haryana boxers.

3. To find out the significant differences of Anthropometric Characteristics (i.e., Standing Height, Weight, Leg Length, Upper Leg Length, Lower Leg Length, Arm Length, Upper Arm Length, Lower Arm Length, Hip Width, Shoulder Width, Chest Width, Calf Girth, Thigh Girth, Chest Girth, Upper Arm Girth and Lower Arm Girth) among Punjab and Haryana boxers.

# HYPOTHESES OF THE STUDY

1. There would be no significant difference of Physical Fitness Components (i.e., Speed, Agility, Balance, Coordination, Reaction Time and Power) among Punjab and Haryana boxers.

2. There would be no significant difference of Physiological Characteristics (i.e., Vital Capacity, Pulse Rate and Peak Flow Rate) among Punjab and Haryana boxers.

3. There would be no significant differences of Anthropometric Characteristics (i.e., Standing Height, Weight, Leg Length, Upper Leg Length, Lower Leg Length, Arm Length, Upper Arm Length, Lower Arm Length, Hip Width, Shoulder Width, Chest Width, Calf Girth, Thigh Girth, Chest Girth, Upper Arm Girth and Lower Arm Girth) among Punjab and Haryana boxers.

# DELIMITATIONS OF THE STUDY

*This study included the following delimitations:*

1. The study was delimited to the Punjab and Haryana male boxers of 19-28 years of age group.

2. The study was further delimited to the Punjab and Haryana male boxers of following weight categories:

| Light Weight | 57-60 |
| Light Welter Weight | 60-64 |
| Welter Weight | 64-69 |
| Middle Weight | 69-75 |

3. The study was delimited to the following Physical, Physiological and Anthropometric Characteristics:

   I.   Physical Fitness Components:

       i.   Speed

       ii.   Agility

       iii.   Balance

       iv.   Coordination

       v.   Reaction Time

       vi.   Power

   II.   Physiological Characteristics:

       i.   Vital Capacity

    ii.     Pulse Rate

    iii.    Peak Flow Rate

III.    Anthropometric Characteristics:

    i.     Standing Height

    ii.    Weight

    iii.   Leg Length

    iv.   Upper Leg Length

    v.    Lower Leg Length

    vi.   Arm Length

    vii.   Upper Arm Length

    viii.  Lower Arm Length

    ix.   Hip Width

    x.    Shoulder Width

    xi.   Chest Width

    xii.   Calf Girth

    xiii.  Thigh Girth

    xiv.  Chest Girth

    xv.   Upper Arm Girth

    xvi.  Lower Arm Girth

## LIMITATIONS OF THE STUDY

*The following limitations restrict the generalizability of the results of this study:*

1. The study was cross-sectional in design, therefore, only comparison among Punjab and Haryana boxers can be made-no casual inferences are possible.

2. A limited diversity existed among the athletes; therefore, the results cannot be generalized into other sports settings

3. Physical fitness is just one component that affects athletic performance. There are a plethora of factors effecting athletic performance including, but not limited to, natural ability, nutrition, sleep, life patterns, etc.

4. External influences affecting athlete's perceptions and physical activity level cannot be controlled for within the control groups.

# DEFINITION & EXPLANATION OF THE TERMS

## Physical Fitness Components

**Speed**

— It has been defined as the capacity of an individual to perform successive movements of the same pattern at a fast rate.

**Agility**

— It has been defined as one's controlled ability to change body position and direction rapidly and accurately.

**Power**

— Power is the capacity of the individual to bring into play maximum muscle contraction at the fastest rate of speed.

**Reaction Time**

— The amount of time required to respond to a stimulus. Typically, stimuli are either visual or auditory.

**Balance**

— A state of equilibrium.

**Coordination**

— The state of being coordinate; harmonious adjustment or interaction.

## Physiological Characteristics

**Vital Capacity**

— Vital capacity is defined as the largest volume of air that can be exhaled followed by deepest possible inhalation.

**Resting Pulse Rate**

— It has been defined as the number of pulse waves per minute felt at the radial artery.

**Peak Flow Rate**

— The peak expiratory flow rate measures how fast a person can breathe out (exhale) air.

# Anthropometric Characteristics

**Anthropometric Measurements**

— An anthropometric measurement is defined as dimensions of the structure of the human body taken at specific sites to give measures of length, girth and width.

**Standing height**

— It is defined as the maximum height of the individual when standing erect on a horizontal surface with his head and face in Frankfurt horizontal plane or it is the straight height of the subject (bare-footed) up to the point vertex.

**Body weight**

— Weight of the nude human body with empty bowels is known as body weight.

**Leg length**

— The leg length has been measured from the greater trochanter (Head of the Femur) to the outside edge of the centre of the foot.

**Upper leg length**

— It is measured from the Iliacspinale to Tibiae.

**Lower leg length**

— It is measured from the Tibiae to the floor.

**Arm length**

— The arm length was taken from the acromion process above the shoulder joint to the tip of the middle finger.

**Upper arm length**

— It is measured at the upper edge of the head of acromiale to the tip of the top of the point of radial.

**Lower arm length**

— It is measured at the upper edge of the head of the radius to the tip of the middle finger.

**Hip width (bitrochantric diameter)**

— It is the straight distance between the right and left trochanterion points. Trochanterion is the most superior and lateral point on the greater trochanter of the femur.

**Shoulder width (biacromial diameter)**

— It is the straight distance between the left and right acromial points. Acromial is the lateral most point on the superior and external border of the acromion process of the scapula.

**Chest width**

— Subject stands erect with his arms initially raised and then lowered after the anthropometer is in place. The width of the chest is measured at the level of the nipples during normal breathing as a horizontal distance.

**Calf girth**

— It is the maximal girth of the lower leg over the calf muscles.

**Thigh girth**

— It is the girth of the thigh at a mid-point of femur length.

**Chest girth**

— It is the maximal girth of the chest, which passes below the lower edge of the scapula and just under the mammilla in front.

**Upper arm girth**

— The girth of freely hanging upper-arm measured mid- way between the point acromiale and the radial.

**Lower arm girth**

— It is the maximal girth of the forearm.

## SIGNIFICANCE OF THE STUDY

*This study was significant for the following reasons:*

1. The results may be used as the predictors for successful performance in Punjab and Haryana male boxers.
2. The findings of this study may give certain guidelines based on basis of Physical, Physiological and Anthropometric Characteristics for selecting an athlete for boxing sports.
3. The findings of this study will be helpful for knowledge regarding the Physical, Physiological and Anthropometric Characteristics in combat sport.
4. The results of the study will give an insight to physical educators, coaches and trainers to understand the role of Physical, Physiological and Anthropometric Characteristics in combat sport .

5. The current study will help in determining the specific difference of Physical, Physiological and Anthropometric Characteristics among Punjab and Haryana male boxers.

6. The results of this study will be of immense support to the sports scientists, physician, teachers and coaches to frame or modify the existing schedules of training.

7. The results of this study may help to find out the potentialities in the area of different sports that help to canalizes students in different games and sports.

8. The study may help in drawing conclusions and generalizations which may be used by physical education teachers and coaches for better teaching and coaching.

## Chapter - II

# Review of Related Literature

## Introduction

A careful review and exploration of the related literature was indispensable to provide ideas, theories, explanation or hypothesis valuable in formulating the problem, to avoid the risk of duplicating the same study already undertaken, to suggest methods of research appropriate to the problem, to locate comparative data useful in the interpretation of results and to contribute to the general scholarship of the investigator. The current chapter was designed to bring light on a few related empirical studies which are relevant to the problem under study.

# CHAPTER-II
# REVIEW OF RELATED LITERATURE

Martin A. Salah (2012) investigated the influence of some anthropometric and physiological factors on performance in the context of the Mount Cameroon Race of Hope. Age, height, weight, blood pressure, heart rate and breathing rate of 83 finisher athletes of both genders were collected during medical check-up, and race time was recorded at the arrival line. Measured and calculated data association with performance was assessed. The race time was significantly influenced by the area of training (p=0.0022), and gender (p=0.0036) of athletes; BMI showed significant association with race time in the overall athletes' population; this was confirmed in male (r=0.565; p=0.034) but not in female athletes (r=0.749; p=0.058). Weight class showed significant association to performance, the lighter athletes performing better than the heavier (p<0.00001). None of the investigated physiological parameters showed association to the race time. It was hypothesized that high altitude training and body size are significantly influential on athletes' performance in the Mount Cameroon race of hope and similar mountain races.

Said (2012) aimed to assess the associations between implementing CMS versus simple motor skill (SMS) training and the subsequent changes in physical, technical and technical performance effectiveness (TPE) variables in junior boxers. We employed an experimental design that comprised two groups (each 20 males, mean age = 15.22±0.62 years). For 12 weeks, intervention boxers received CMS training, while controls received traditional SMS training. Physical, technical and TPE variables were measured before and after the training programs. Although the two groups were of similar abilities at baseline, there were statistically significant differences (P<0.05) between the intervention and control boxers in the post measures, to the advantage of the intervention group. In terms of absolute (i.e. differences in) or relative (i.e. ratios of) improvements, the intervention group exhibited more favourable values across the variables, and better performance. Developing CMS of junior boxers could contribute positively to their physical and technical abilities, and enhance their TPE.

Said El Ashker (2012) aimed to assess the associations between implementing CMS versus simple motor skill (SMS) training and the subsequent changes in physical, technical and technical performance effectiveness (TPE) variables in junior boxers. We employed an experimental design that comprised two groups (each 20 males, mean age = $15.22\pm0.62$ years). For 12 weeks, intervention boxers received CMS training, while controls received traditional SMS training. Physical, technical and TPE variables were measured before and after the training programs. Although the two groups were of similar abilities at baseline, there were statistically significant differences ($P<0.05$) between the intervention and control boxers in the post measures, to the advantage of the intervention group. In terms of absolute (i.e. differences in) or relative (i.e. ratios of) improvements, the intervention group exhibited more favourable values across the variables, and better performance. Developing CMS of junior boxers could contribute positively to their physical and technical abilities, and enhance their TPE.

Said El-Ashker (2012) aimed to assess the effects of boxing exercises on physiological and biochemical responses of Egyptian elite boxers. Seventeen Egyptian elite male boxers (age range 18-23 years) registered in the Egyptian boxing federation, volunteered to participate in the study. Physiological and biochemical measures were obtained at baseline and at the end of boxing training programme. Student's (T) test was followed out to examine pre- and post-test values. Data noted that boxing exercises were associated with significant decreases ($p < 0.05$) in resting heart rate (HRrest), recovery heart rate after 1 minute (RHR1st), recovery heart rate after 2 minutes (RHR2nd), recovery heart rate after 3 minutes (RHR3rd), respiratory exchange ratio (RER) values, and blood lactate (BL) concentration, while they connected with significant increases ($p < 0.05$) in peak heart rate (HRPeak), relative and absolute VO2Max, Creatine Kinase (CK) and Lactate Dehydrogenase (LDH) values. The authors' statistics demonstrate considerable physiological and biochemical changes significantly affected by boxing exercises in elite boxers. Examining relationships connected with the effects of training on physiological and biochemical aspects add new dimensions that can help in assessing, directing and developing athletic training programme.

Said El Ashker (2011) analysised of video recordings of boxing matches could verify differentiation between winners and losers. The aim of this study was to determine aspects of winning and losing boxers based on the use of technical and tactical elements over the progression of boxing contests and differences through bouts. A Sample of 66 first-ranked male elite boxers (aged 22.1 ± 2.3) in 33 fights (11finals; 22 semi-finals) was used. Nineteen variables were determined to describe technical and tactical elements within boxing matches. Differences between rounds were examined by a combined 3 x 2 within and between factors ANOVA to identify main effects through rounds as within winners or losers, with Bonferroni post-hoc analysis. Results showed that winners were higher developed than losers in performing offensive skills directed to head or body, total, lead and rear hand punches, boxing combinations, defensive skills and technical performance effectiveness (TPE) statistics. Data emphasizes the significance of making more punches in both single punches and in combinations in order to score more points than the opponent. Defensive skills should be utilized by arm, foot and trunk connected with attack. Prospective studies need to be considered to investigate the association between performance and physiological and biomechanical variables.

Carlos & Rita (2012) investigated the factors associated to the physical inactivity among teenagers in Salvador, BA. A cross-sectional study was made with 803 teenagers from 10 to 14 years old, enrolled in public high schools in Salvador, BA. Information concerning physical activity levels (dependent variable), sedentary behaviour, demographic, anthropometric, socioeconomic and maternal characteristics (independent variables) were collected. The Poisson multivariate analysis was chosen to analyze the statistical data. The prevalence of physical inactivity was 49,6% (CI 95% 46,14 - 53,06); with higher standards between females (girls: 59,9%; boys: 39%, p < 0,001). With the multivariate analyses, it was verified a inverse association between physical inactivity and family economical condition that was classified in D/E $_{worse\ economical\ levels}$ either among males (PR = 0,73, CI 95%, 0,54 - 0,046), as among females (PR = 0,79; CI 95%; 0,66 - 0,96). In complementary analysis according to domains of physical activity, It was observed a significant decrease of physical inactivity in displacement domain between teenagers of lower economical levels (Boys - Classes B1/B2/C1 = 20,6%, C2 = 11%, D/E = 6%, p = 0,001; Girls - Classes B1/B2/C1 = 26,7%, C2 = 12,5%, D/E = 10,8%, p = 0,003). The prevalence of

15

physical inactivity is high among the studied teenagers. Youths with lower economical levels are more active comparing with those with higher economical standards. Moreover, the association between physical activity and economical condition is influenced by physical activity domain that was investigated.

Anna-Liisa (2011) study to investigate the relationships between specific anthropometric (9 skinfolds, 13 girths, 8 lengths and 8 breadths), body composition (body fat %, fat free mass [FFM], fat mass [FM]) parameters and bone mineral parameters (bone mineral density [BMD], bone mineral content [BMC) in young rhythmic gymnasts and same age controls. Eighty nine 7-8-year-old girls participated in this study and were divided to the rhythmic gymnast's (n = 46) and control (n = 43) groups. Body composition was determined by dual energy X-ray absorptiometry (FFM, FM, body fat %, BMD and BMC). Body fat % and FM were lower and BMD and BMC values at lumbar spine (L2-L4) and femoral neck were higher in rhythmic gymnasts compared with controls. All measured skinfold thicknesses were thicker in controls. In girths, lengths and widths there were only few significant differences between the groups. Stepwise multiple regression analysis indicated that skinfold thicknesses (supraspinale and medial calf) influenced L2-L4 BMD only in controls 38.2%(R2x100). Supraspinale and iliac crest skinfold thicknesses characterised L2-L4 BMC 43.9%(R2x100). Calf girths influenced BMD in L2-L4 52.3%(R2x100) in controls. BMC in L2-L4 was dependent only on mid-thigh girths 35.9%(R2x100). BMD in L2-L4 was dependent on tibiale-laterale height 30.0%(R2x100). Biiliocristal breadths together with sitting height characterised BMC in L2-L4 BMD 62.3%(R2x100). In conclusion, we found that the relationships between anthropometry, body composition and bone parameters in young rhythmic gymnasts are weak. In control group first of all lower body anthropometric parameters significantly correlated with BMD and BMC in spine.

Santhiago et al. (2011) conducted a study to investigate the influence of a 14-week swimming training program on psychological, hormonal, and performance parameters of elite women swimmers. Ten Olympic and international-level elite women swimmers were evaluated 4 times along the experiment (i.e., in T1, T2, T3, and T4). On the first day at 8:00 am, before the blood collecting at rest for the determination of hormonal parameters, the athletes had their psychological parameters assessed by the profile of mood-state questionnaire. At 3:00 am, the swimmers had their anaerobic threshold assessed. On the second day at 3:00 am, the athletes had their alactic anaerobic performance measured. Vigor score and testosterone levels were lower ($p \leq 0.05$) in T4 compared with T3. In addition, the rate between the peak blood lactate concentration and the median velocity obtained in the alactic anaerobic performance test increased in T4 compared with T3 ($p \leq 0.05$). For practical applications, the swimming coaches should not use a tapering with the present characteristics to avoid unexpected results.

Cuesta-Vargas et al. (2011) conducted a study to describe the physical fitness profile of adult athletes with ID and identify whether there are differences in the physical performance between the most physically active individuals and less active individuals. A cross-sectional observational study was developed involving 266 athletes with mild ID (187 males and 79 females), recruited from the Spanish Special Olympics Games. A questionnaire was used to evaluate the health status of participants and their frequency of physical activity practice. A battery of 13 fitness tests was applied to assess flexibility, strength/endurance, balance and cardiovascular capabilities. Of the total participants, 44.3% were classified as sportspersons and the remainder as non sportspersons, taking in consideration the frequency of physical activity. The findings in this study illustrate an unclear and inconclusive relation between the scores and the declared level of physical activity, maybe due to the context in which participants for the study were selected.

Gaurav et al. (2011) investigate the significant differences of selected physical fitness variables between individual games and team games athletes. A group of 30 sportspersons A (Individual games athletes: N=15) and B (Team games athletes=15) of age group 18-25 years were selected from department of physical education (T), Guru Nanak Dev University, Amritsar, Punjab, India. It was hypothesized that there may be significant differences with regard to selected physical fitness variables among individual and team games athletes. The between-group differences were assessed by using an independent samples t-test. The level of $p \leq 0.01$ was considered significant. An independent samples t-test revealed that individual games athletes had significantly higher muscular strength, agility, power, speed and cardiovascular endurance ($p < 0.01$) than team games athletes. Further investigations are needed on the above studied variables along with physiological variables to assess relationships among them and with performances in team games and individual games athletes.

Giovani (2012) conducted a study on the physiology or the biomechanics of this sport. The aim of the present study is to examine the ratios of mechanical characteristics (maximal anaerobic power, Pmax, theoretical maximal force, F0, and velocity, v0) between upper and lower limbs of male boxers. Twelve male Caucasians, all members of a local fitness club, aged 29.5 (3.2) yr [mean (standard deviation)], stature 1.74 (.05) m, body mass 77.9 (8.1) kg, body fat 22.4 (3.9) % and somatotype 5.5- 5.5-1.1, performed a force-velocity (F-v) test for both legs and arms. The F-v test included five supramaximal pedal sprints, each lasting 7 sec, against incremental braking force of 20-60 N for arms and 30-70 N for legs, on modified arm-cranking and on cycle ergometer (Ergomedics 874, Monark, Sweden). The legs had higher Pmax (910 W vs. 445 W, $t11$=22.9, $p$<.001), Pmax expressed in relative to body mass values (rPmax, 11.8 W.kg-1 vs. 5.8 W.kg-1, $t11$=20.6,$p$<.001), F0 (168 N vs. 102 N, $t11$=21.7, $p$<.001), v0 (217 rpm vs. 177 rpm, $t11$=46.6, $p$<.001) and lower v0/F0 (1.33 rpm.N-1 vs. 1.82 rpm.N-1, $t11$=15.3, $p$<.001) than the arms. Pmax of upper limbs was associated with Pmax of lower limbs ($r$=.70, $p$<.05) and their ratio was .49 (.06). The respective values of rPmax was $r$=.76 ($p$<.01), F0, $r$=.35 ($p$=.26) and .61 (.13), and of velocity, v0,$r$=.17 ($p$=.59) and .812 (.10). In spite of moderate associations between upper and lower limbs' F0 and v0, a stronger relationship was found with regard to Pmax. These findings emphasize the need for separate evaluation of arms' and legs' F-v characteristics on a regular basis and the consideration of these measures in training design.

Vishav et al. (2011) conducted a study to compare the somatic traits and body composition between volleyball players and controls. 48 young male subjects (volleyball players: N= 24 & controls: N= 24) of age group 18-25 years were randomly selected from the different colleges affiliated to Guru Nanak Dev University, Amritsar, Punjab, India. All the participants were assessed for height, weight, breadths, girths and skin fold thickness. The independent samples t-test revealed that volleyball players had significantly higher height (p<0.05), as compared to controls. The volleyball players were also found to have significantly greater lean body mass (p<0.01) and ectomorphic component (p<0.05) as compared to controls.

Controls had significantly greater percent body fat and total body fat ($p<0.05$) as compared to volleyball players. The volleyball players of this study were found to have higher percentage body fat with lower body height and body weight than their international counterparts. Further investigations are needed on above studied variables along with fitness and physiological variables to assess relationship among them and with performance in volleyball. The findings of the present study might be useful in future investigation on player selection, talent identification in the game of volleyball and its training programme development.

Gilenstam et al. (2011) conducted a study to identify relationships between physiological off-ice tests and on-ice performance in female and male ice hockey players on a comparable competitive level. Eleven women, $24 \pm 3.0$ years, and 10 male ice hockey players, $23 \pm 2.4$ years, were tested for background variables: height, body weight (BW), ice hockey history, and lean body mass (LBM) and peak torque (PT) of the thigh muscles, &OV0312; o2peak and aerobic performance (Onset of Blood Lactate Accumulation [OBLA], respiratory exchange ratio [RER1]) during an incremental bicycle ergo meter test. Four different on-ice tests were used to measure ice skating performance. For women, skating time was positively correlated ($p < 0.05$) to BW and negatively correlated to LBM%, PT/BW, OBLA, RER 1, and &OV0312; o2peak (ml O2·kg BW·min) in the Speed test. Acceleration test was positively correlated to BW and negatively correlated to OBLA and RER 1. For men, correlation analysis revealed only 1 significant correlation where skating time was positively correlated to &OV0312; o2peak (L O2·min) in the Acceleration test. The male group had significantly higher physiological test values in all variables (absolute and relative to BW) but not in relation to LBM. Selected off-ice tests predict skating performance for women but not for men.

Ghorbanzadeh (2011) studied to establish the physical and physiological attributes of elite and subelite Turkish male and female taekwondo players and to determine whether these attributes discriminate elite players from sub-elite players. Measurements and tests of basic anthropometry, explosive power, anaerobic recovery capacity arm strength, were conducted on two occasions, separated by at least one day. The research has been carried out with 24 men and 16 women successful Turkish National Team taekwondo athletes who have had degrees in European and World

Championships several times, and 24 male and 16 female ordinary athletes who have not been in National Teams. 81 subjects have taken part in this research. In the research, totally 31 physical and anthropometric variables have been analysed by testing. In comparing the data obtaining from the athletes who were and were not in National Teams in free groups,'t' test; and as for determining the statistical relations between the anthropometric and physical characteristics, Pearson Correlation analyze statistics has been used. In analyzing the results, the signifance level has been accepted as (p<0.05).

Nudri (2010) conducted to determine the anthropometric measurements and body composition of selected national athletes. A total of 84 male athletes from 10 different types of sports and 24 female athletes from 5 types of sports were studied. The height and body weight of subjects were measured using the SEGA weighing balance with height attachment. Skinfold thickness measurements were taken using the Harpenden Calipers at 4 sites (biceps, triceps, subscapular and suprailiac). Percentage of body fat was calculated from the sum of 4 measurements of skinfold thickness. Based on body mass index (BMI), most of the male (68 subjects or 81%) and female (19 subjects or 79%) athletes were classified as normal. The percentage average body fat for both male and female athletes were $13.8 \pm 4.5\%$ and $24.7 \pm 5.3\%$, respectively. The male and female athletes also had lower percentage of body fat when compared to non-athletes, however these athletes had slightly higher percentage of body fat when compared to those in selected countries.

Ismail (2010) examined within the middleweight class, the relationship between ranking in boxing competition performance and some physiological factors. Eight elite Italian amateur boxers (first series of AIBA ranking) were assessed in 2 testing sessions, a week apart. In the first testing session all subjects underwent anthropometric measurements from which body fat percentage, upper arm and forearm muscle cross-sectional areas were estimated. In the second testing session all subjects performed grip strength measures and a maximal treadmill test to assess oxygen consumption (VO2), blood lactate and heart rate at maximal effort, at individual anaerobic threshold, and at individual ventilatory threshold. The athletes were ranked following the criteria of world amateur AIBA ranking. In this ranking the first ranked boxer had the highest score gained participating in international tournaments.A Spearman rho correlation analysis revealed that the VO2 at individual anaerobic threshold (46.0+/-4.2 ml x kg(-1) x min(-1), r=0.91) and the hand-grip strength (58.2+/-6.9 kg, r=0.87) were highly related (p<0.01) to boxing competition ranking. VO(2max) (57.5+/-4.7 ml x kg(-1) x min(-1), r=0.81) and wrist girth (17.6+/-0.6 cm, r=0.78) were moderately (p<0.05) related. These data suggest that there are two basic factors related to boxing performance: physical fitness as indicated by individual anaerobic threshold and maximal oxygen consumption, and upper-body muscular strength as indicated by hand-grip strength. Bottom of Form

Chandrasekhar et al. (2010) determined the physiological capacities, different physiological parameters like body weight , height, blood pressure, body density, body mass index, body surface area, body fat %, lean body mass, hand grip strength, hand grip endurance, maximal aerobic capacity and anaerobic power were compared in wrestler. Wrestler undergoing training, were in the age group of 18-25 year. Statistical analysis was done using ANOVA test and tukey's test. Hand grip strength, hand grip endurance, endurance in 40 mm Hg test, maximal aerobic capacity and lean body mass increased with increase duration of training.

Charilaos et al. (2010) aimed at investigating the differences in selected anthropometric, strength ‑ power parameters and functional characteristics of fencing performance between elite and sub ‑ elite fencers. Thirty ‑ three fencers (18 females and 15 males) from the Greek National Team, (age 19 ± 3.5 yr, body height 175.6 ± 7.6 cm, body mass 66.1 ± 9.1 kg, systematic training 8.4 ± 2.9 yr) were classified as elite and sub ‑ elite, according to their international experience. Subjects underwent a detailed anthropometric assessment and performed selected leg power and fencing specific tests. Significant differences were observed between the two groups in sitting height, triceps, sub scapular, and quadriceps dominant skin fold thickness, absolute and body mass ‑ dependent expressions of leg functional power characteristics of fencing performance: "time of lunge" and time of the "shuttle test". Anthropometric traits, such as height, body mass, percent fat and limb lengths were not different among elite and sub ‑ elite fencers. Although technical and tactical factors are good indicators of fencing success, the observed differences in functional fencing performance tests among different levels of fencers are useful for the design of effective talent development and training conditioning programs for competitive fencers.

Sisodiya et al. (2010) aimed to determine the relationship between anthropometric Measurements to the playing ability in basketball (jonshon basketball test). 50 male and 50 female basketball national level players of Rajasthan state were selected as subject for the purpose of this study. Present study exhibited the insignificant relationship with field goal speed test (basketball playing ability) and with throw for accuracy at the chosen level but the value of product moment correlation is quite higher which may be understood that the size of body may contribute to basketball playing ability when combined with other variables. Finding of study show the insignificant relationship between body weight and basketball playing ability which may be attribute to the fact that basketball players do not require bulky body which may hidden the performance of the players. The findings reveal that insignificant relationship exist between let length and Field ball speed test and dribble test (basketball playing ability) no significant relationship was found with throw ball accuracy. It is because of the fact that a leg with a good length but without explosive strength to be contributing factors for speed and jumping ability which is required for performing with in basketball game.

Gaurav et al. (2010) carried out a study to compare the anthropometric characteristics and somatotype of the Guru Nanak Dev University, Amritsar's male basketball players and volleyball players. Sixty three sportspersons (volleyball=36 and basketball=27) of age group 18-25 years were selected from different colleges affiliated to Guru Nanak Dev University, Amritsar, Punjab, India. All the participants were assessed for height, weight, breadths, girths and skin fold thickness. An independent samples t-test revealed that basketball players had significantly higher height (p<0.01), weight (p<0.01) and body surface area (p<0.01) as compared to volleyball players. The basketball players were also found to have significantly greater biceps (p<0.01) and suprailliac (p<0.01) skin fold thicknesses, calf circumference (p<0.05), percent body fat (p<0.01), total body fat (p<0.01), fat free mass (p<0.05) and endomorphic component (p<0.05) as compared to volleyball players. Volleyball players had significantly greater body density (p<0.01) as compared to basketball players. The basketball and volleyball players of this study were found to have higher percentage body fat with lower body height and body weight than their international counterparts. Further investigations are needed on the above studied variables along with fitness and physiological variables to assess relationships among them and with performances in volleyball and basketball.

Mohamed (2010) conducted a study to find out the important anthropometry measurements, which represent the basic dimensions of the body in sports, volleyball and handball, from Egyptian juniors in the age from 15 to 18 years. The research sample included 61 juniors, divided into 25 juniors of volleyball and 36 for handball. Selecting the research sample was by using of the method of random sample and included a sample of some Egyptian juniors in volleyball and handball, registered in Egyptian sports federations of the two sports. The researcher applied the 44 anthropometry variables under study on a pilot study, on the number of 30 juniors were selected from junior and outside the sample basic research and that was at 15 juniors of volleyball, 15 juniors of handball and be credited to the validity and reliability of the measurements of anthropometric, has made transactions stability elevated limited between 1 to 0.934, and all statistically significant at 0.01 level, which indicates the stability of measurements and conclusions, the researcher recommends that the anthropometric measurements, resulted from the current study, are among the most important foundations which take into account when choosing players of volleyball and handball.

Pichini et al (2010) examined a study aimed to studied that the Indirect biomarkers of recombinant human growth hormone (rhGH), insulin-like growth factor-I (IGF-I), insulin-like growth factor-II (IGF-II), insulin-like growth factor binding proteins (IGFBP-2 and IGFBP-3) and insulin (C-peptide) were measured together with urinary parameters of renal damage (beta(2)-macroglobulin and proteinuria) by immunoassays, in house validated for the purpose, in 61 subjects (36 elite athletes, 18 recreational athletes and 7 sedentary individuals) with different levels of physical fitness and endurance exercise. Among elite athletes, tae-kwon-do athletes showed the highest IGF-II basal values while weightlifting athletes showed the lower IGF-I and IGFBP-3 basal values. The trend observed in weightlifters' basal samples was confirmed in their training samples: IGF-I, IGF-II, IGFBP-3 and beta (2) macroglobulins were lower in with respect to those from synchronized swimming.

Over the training season, within athlete variability was observed for IGFBP-3 for weightlifting athletes. In the studied subjects, no direct associations were found between biomarkers of GH or insulin misuse and urinary parameters of renal damage, eventually due to high-workload endurance training. The variations observed in different biomarkers should be taken in consideration in the hypothesis of setting reference concentration ranges for doping detection.

Wisniewski et al. (2010) conducted a study to determine the Physical activity is regarded as one of the four basic factors influencing the concentration of glucose in the blood of diabetic patients. Despite this, concerns about hypoglycemia and exposure of chronically ill children to excessive fatigue mean that their physical activity is frequently inadequate. Until now, physical endurance of diabetes mellitus patients has been assessed more frequently than their physical fitness. Monroe CM, et al.(2010)  This study examined the relation of college students' self-perceived and measured physical fitness. Students (30 men, 30 women; M age = 20.1 yr., SD = 1.4) completed the Physical Self-description Questionnaire and four fitness tests: air displacement plethysmography, sub maximal treadmill test, curl-up test, and sit-and-reach test. Significant correlations were obtained for self-perceived physical fitness with measured body composition, cardio respiratory endurance, muscular endurance, and flexibility (r = .33-.62). Significant correlations were also found between self-perceived overall fitness and actual body composition, cardio respiratory endurance, and muscular endurance (|r| = .26-.55). These findings suggest that college students can gauge their own fitness in terms of four distinct health-related components with some accuracy.

Fong et al. (2010) investigated that Taekwondo (TKD) is a popular sport practiced by people of all ages in more than 180 countries and it is generally considered as being beneficial to health even though the scientific evidence for this is not conclusive. The main outcomes examined were anaerobic and aerobic fitness body composition, muscle strength, endurance, power and flexibility. Results There are no conclusive evidence in the literature that TKD practice can improve anaerobic fitness or muscle strength. However, TKD training may have some benefits in aerobic capacity, body composition (fat loss) and flexibility. Conclusion

Physiotherapists or fitness instructors may consider recommending TKD to their clients as a beneficial form of exercise to promote aerobic fitness and flexibility.

Roy et al. (2010) assess the selected physical and physiological characteristics of elite male and female marathon runners of Manipur and compare the results with male and female marathon runner of Manipur and compare the results with that of the elite marathon runners of other countries. Twelve elite marathon runner of Manipur, including females, who represented the country at least once, or participated and won at least a medal, in the national or international level were enrolled to assess their physical and physiological parameters like body composition, strength and maximal aerobic power. It was found that the mean body weight and height of the male marathon runners were 57.2 kg and 166.7 cm. respectively; whereas, those of the female counterparts were 41.8,kg and 156.6 cm. respectively. The mean fat % for the male runners was 8.9%; whereas, that of the female counterparts was 15.1 %. The mean fat free mass, for the males and female, was 52.0 kg and 35.5 kg, respectively. The mean strength of the quadriceps, at 30 % speed, was 164.3 Nm for males and 128.2 Nm for females and that of the hamstrings was 137.5 Nm and 78.9 Nm for males and females respectively. The maximal aerobic power were similar among both groups of runners with both recording a mean VO2 max recordable value of 85.3 ml kg min. on comparison with the elite marathon runners of other countries it was found that the marathon runners of Manipur were yet to develop ideal physique and body composition, to achieve reasonable success, at the international level. The high maximal aerobic power among the runners may be advantageous in developing international level athletes; and there for, the emphasis should be on proper systematic and scientific training of athletes, utilizing the high VO2 max, from the grass root level, with subsequent adequate exposure is the international meets.

Sangha (2010) determined and compared physical fitness level and personality traits among male wrestlers across there level of participation. A random sampling of 150 male wrestlers was selected from colleges and universities of Haryana, at different level of participation i.e. inter-college, inter-district and inter-university/ national level, between the age group of 18 to 25 years. The data were collected through AAPHER fitness test revised (1976). And cattell's 16 personality factor questionnaire (1968). It has been observed and concluded that all the three groups significantly differ on six variables / components of physical fitness namely pull-up, sit up, shuttle run, standing broad jump, 50 yard desh and 600 yard run. Dimensions of personality traits were found at significant level, among all the three groups, at various level of confidence. It was found that physical fitness and performance were too much co-related with each other. Personality traits of tough mindedness, ego, strength, assertiveness, emotional stability, intelligence, will power and self confidence are help full in better performance of wrestlers. It has been observe that high achiever wrestlers need stress management strategies, along with consideration of individuality, in team composition. Physical fitness and psychological make up, systematic training and there knowledge essential spots behavior, which add in optimum level of performance.

Kapoor et al. (2010) compared anthropometric and physiological parameter of young wrestler grouped by training duration. 60 male wrestlers attending a wrestling training school at youth service and spots center, Davangere, were tested to determine their physiological capacities. Different physiological parameter like body weight, height, blood pressure, body density, body mass index, body surface area, body fat %, lean body mass, hand grip strength, hand grip endurance, maximum aerobic capacity, and anaerobic power were compared in wrestlers. Wrestlers undergoing training were in the age group of 18-25 year. They had participated at state and national level competition [elite wrestler] and presently undergoing training youth services and sports center, davangere. These specific age group wrestlers were in different duration of training. statistical analysis was done using ANOVA test and tukey's test. Hand grip strength, hand grip endurance, endurance in 40 mm Hg test, maximal aerobic capacity and lean body mass increased with increased duration of training. Effect of training to evaluate training schedule and to assess efficiency and/or potentiality of different groups of trained wrestler, can be compared with this study.

Almeida and Abreu (2010) assess the dietetic and anthropometric profiles of 25 female adolescent volleyball players of Rio de Janeiro (15-20 years old). Anthropometric assessment was obtained by body mass, stature, skinfold and circumference measurements. Prospective 3-day records that include two weekdays and one weekend day were analyzed by a Brazilian nutrition software (CIS/EPM, 1993) to obtain the nutrient intake and the results were compared to the American recommendations. The results of anthropometric evaluation showed that athletes had body mass of 64.35 ± 6.12 kg, stature of 1.74 ± 0.06 m and fat mass of 20.51 ± 2.43%. Diets consisted of high energy and protein intake, and low carbohydrate intake. The consumption of calcium, folate and vitamin E was below the recommendations. Since these athletes are going through a period of intense growth and development associated with rigorous training, it becomes, therefore, necessary for them to receive individualized nutritional orientation to improve their performance and quality of life.

Helina (2009) conducted a study to determine the relationship of anthropometric and physical fitness variable with handball performance. Handball is the game of applied athletics and it requires well proportionate physique and great amount of physical fitness level. To achieve the objectives of the study six anthropometric and seven physical fitness variables and playing ability as dependent variables, which was assessed through subjective rating, by three experts, during the tournaments and the average was taken as criterion score. Forty five male handball players who had participated the university tournaments. The result of the study was anthropometric variable and physical fitness component were having significant relationship with handball performance and only flexible was not having significant relationship with handball performance.

Zhang (2010) studied to determine the anthropometric characteristics of eliteChinese women volleyball players, identify the differences in the anthropometric profile and physical performance between the players at different volleyball positions,and examine the correlations between the anthropometric profile and the physicalperformance of the players. Thirty-one anthropometric indices and four physicalperformance (medicine ball throwing, running vertical jump, T shuttle run agility testand timed 20 sit ups) were measured for 100 volleyball players recruited from the top eight teams of 2007-2008 national championship. The average age of the players was22.3±3.6 (SD) years and the average training age was 9.7±4.0 years. For the eliteChinese women volleyball players, the average values of stature, body mass, sitting height, standing reach height, and BMI were respectively 183.6±5.8 cm, 70.5±7.6 kg,95.7±3.5 cm, 236.7±7.8 cm, and 20.9±2.0. The overall anthropometric characteristics of these volleyball players can be described as high stature; relatively longer forearm, palm, calf and Achilles' tendon lengths but a shorter sitting height; wider femur,biiliocristal and biacromial breadths; larger difference between relaxed and tensed armgirth, smaller wrist and ankle girths, smaller ankle girth / Achilles' tendon length index; and smaller skinfolds. The results also revealed that most of the anthropometric variables were poorly correlated with the selected physical performance measurements, except that the biepicondylar femur breadth, calf girth and calf length indices were significantly correlated with the running jump height. There were significant differences among the anthropometric profiles of the players at different volleyball positions, especially in the indices of body mass, stature, standing reach height, radiale-stylion length, acromiale-dactylion length, midstylion-dactylion length,iliospinale height, tibiale-laterale height length, biacromial breadth, biiliocristal breadth,transverse chest breadth and gluteal girth (all $P<0.001$). However, the physicalperformance of the players at different positions showed no significant between-position difference except the running jump height. The average somatoype values of elite Chinese women volleyball players were "3.7-2.9-4.0", belonging to endomorph-ectomorph. Their somatoypes were found mainly in four of the 13categories, with 29% in endomorphic ectomorph, 14% in balanced ectomorph, 11% in balanced endomorph and 9% in ectomorph-endomorph. The somatotype of the spikersand liberos was of the central type, that of the second spikers and second setters was endomorphic ectomorph, and that of the setters was endomorph-ectomorph. Based on the findings of this study, it is recommended that the following anthropometric indicesbe considered in recruitment for women volleyball players: body mass, stature, sitting height, biacromial breadth, subscapular skinfold, ankle girth, forearm girth and Achilles' tendon length.

Gopinath et al. (2009) studied to determine the relationship of anthropometric and physical fitness variables with handball performance. Handball is a game of applied athletics and it requires well proportionate physique and great amount of physical fitness level. To achieve the objectives of the study six anthropometric and seven physical fitness variables were included as independent variables and playing ability as dependent variable, which was assessed through subjective rating, by three experts, during the tournaments and the average was taken as criterion score, forty five male handball players, who had participated the university of madras handball tournament in 2007-08 season were selected as subjects. Pearson's product moment correlation (zero order) was used as a statistical tool to find out the result and it revealed that the anthropometric variables of height, weight, arm length, leg length, palm span and sum of four skin folds and physical fitness variables or speed, agility, explosive power, shoulder strength, strength endurance and endurance were having significant relationship with handball performance and only flexibility was not having significant relationship with handball performance.

Gall et al. (2009) examined a study to compared anthropometric and fitness performance data from graduate male youth players from an elite soccer academy who on leaving the institution were either successful or not in progressing to higher standards of play. Altogether, 161 players were grouped according to whether they achieved international or professional status or remained amateur. Measures were taken across three age categories (under 14, 15 and 16 years of age). Players were assessed using standard measures of anthropometric and fitness characteristics. The skeletal age of players was also measured to determine maturity status. Multivariate analysis (MANCOVA) identified a significant ($p < 0.001$) effect for playing status. Univariate analysis revealed a significant difference in maturity status in amateurs and professionals versus internationals ($p < 0.05$), in body mass in professionals versus amateurs ($d = 0.56$, $p < 0.05$), in height ($d = 0.85$, $p < 0.01$) and maximal anaerobic power ($d = 0.79$, $p < 0.01$) in both professionals and internationals versus amateurs. These results suggest that anthropometric and fitness assessments of elite youth soccer players can play a part in determining their chances of proceeding to higher achievement levels.

Roopakala et al. (2009) carried out a study to assess the Central obesity is known to be an important risk factor in the development of metabolic syndrome and intra abdominal fat thickness has been found to be a reliable indicator of central obesity. Many anthropometric indicators have been suggested for measuring intra abdominal fat. The aim of this study was to relate various anthropometric measurements to intra abdominal fat thickness and to determine which among these is a better predictor of intra abdominal fat in normal subjects. This cross sectional study was carried out. In 60 healthy subjects (32 males and 28 females) in the age group of 25–55 years. Anthropometric measurements such as BMI, waist circumference and waist-hip ratio were assessed by using standard methods. Subcutaneous and visceral fat were measured 1 cm above umbilicus by ultra sonography. Intra abdominal fat thickness was correlated with the anthropometric measures by Pearson's test. Multivariate linear regression test was used to find the best anthropometric measurement as a predictor of abdominal fat. Waist circumference showed a significant positive correlation with subcutaneous fat and visceral fat. Waist circumference was found to be the best predictor of intra abdominal fat thickness in normal subjects and therefore of central obesity.

Gray and Geraint (2009) studied to compare selected physiological variables and performance markers of soldiers from two "elite" units of the British Army. Ten soldiers from each of the two units were recruited for this study (n = 20). All participants completed three tests while carrying a 20 kg backpack load:(1) a maximal treadmill test using the Bruce protocol;(2) a 2 mile backpack run test specific to Unit A on a consistently flat tarmac road; and (3) a 29 km time-trial over hilly terrain typical of a mountainous area used by Unit B for performance assessment. Heart rate, maximal blood lactate concentration and performance (run time) were assessed during all three tests, with peak oxygen uptake also being measured during the maximal treadmill test. Measurements of anthropometry, isokinetic strength and mental toughness (MT48) were also recorded. There were no significant differences in terms of performance markers between the units (P > 0.05). Performance on the maximal treadmill test correlated with performance on the 2 mile backpack run test (r =-0.57) and 29 km time-trial (r =-0.66). Performance on the 2 mile backpack run test in turn correlated with 29 km time-trial performance (r =-0.77), accounting for 59% of the variance. In conclusion, the maximal treadmill test and the 2 mile backpack run test are useful indicators of performance on the arduous hill march and could be employed in the screening and selection of potential recruits.

Sidhu (2009) conducted a study on 100 boxers and 100 athletes in the age range of 15-25 years to compare their anthropometric characteristics. The subjects were taken from various colleges of Punjab namely Guru Kanshi College, Nehru Memorial College, Mansa, Barjindra College, Faridkot, Rajindra College, Bhatinda. The results of the study in general reveal that boxers are bulky, taller and heavier than athletes; the significant differences however were noted in chest circumference between the two groups. Boxers in general are found to possess more deposition of subcutaneous fat in the regions of biceps, triceps and calf than the athletic group. However in statistical terms it is significant only in the triceps and calf regions. Comparison has also been made between senior and junior athletes and boxers by dividing the subjects into 15-20 and 20-25 year age groups.

Musulin and Baldari (2008) examined, within the middleweight class, the relationship between ranking in boxing competition performance and some physiological factors.|Eight elite Italian amateur boxers (first series of AIBA ranking) were assessed in 2 testing sessions, a week apart. In the first testing session all subjects underwent anthropometric measurements from which body fat percentage, upper arm and forearm muscle cross-sectional areas were estimated. In the second testing session all subjects performed grip strength measures and a maximal treadmill test to assess oxygen consumption (VO2), blood lactate and heart rate at maximal effort, at individual anaerobic threshold, and at individual ventilatory threshold. The athletes were ranked following the criteria of world amateur AIBA ranking. In this ranking the first ranked boxer had the highest score gained participating in international tournaments. A Spearman rho correlation analysis revealed that the VO2 at individual anaerobic threshold (46.0+/-4.2 ).

Varamenti et al. (2008) carried out a study to assess to known that stimuli are presented during training, which lead to biological and functional adaptations, as well as to morphological alterations. The purpose of this study was to determine which of the above characteristics make athletes of the senior women's national team differ from those of the junior women's national team. The two samples of the present study were composed, respectively, of 13 athletes of the women's national team with 9.8 ± 3 years of training experience in the 26.3 ± 4.4 age group (2nd position in the Athens Olympics of 2004) and 13 athletes of the junior women's national team with 6.5 ± 1.7 years of training experience in the 17 ± 1.2 age group (4th position in the Junior European Championship of 2005). Senior female water polo players didn't differ in basic anthropometric variables when compared to the junior female players but only in limited variables. While considerably, they differed more in VO2max (50.3 ± 4.5 vs 45.3 ± 6.8 ml·kg-1·min-1), in performance in 400 m free swimming (5:24 ± 0:16 vs 5:36 ± 0:12 min:sec), in maximal lactate accumulation (8.4 ± 0.7 vs 6.4 ± 1.8 mmol·l-1), in performance in 25 free swimming (13.8 ± 0.4 vs 14.7 ± 0.8 sec), in overhead throwing velocity (16.0 ± 0.6 vs. 15.1 ± 0.5 m·s-1) and on water vertical jump (62.0 ± 2.7 vs. 59.3 ± 3.0 cm), probably due to more intense and more specialized training.

Singh et al (2008) found out the difference in selected anthropometric and fitness variables in basketball players of selected age groups. The subject was divided into 16 year, 17 year, and 18 year age groups. In addition to height and weight measurements, standing broad jump, standing vertical jump, 20 meter run, 6 X 10 shuttle run, and 1500 meter run fitness tests were used to collect data ANOVA was applied to find out the difference among selected groups and post hoc test was applied to find out the paired mean difference in case the 'F' ratio was found significant difference. A difference, in mean value, has been found in adjacent age groups. A significant difference in height and weight variables and a non-significant difference among selected groups, in fitness variables, have been observed.

Varament et al (2008) presented a stimuli during training, which lead to biological and functional adaptations, as well as to morphological alterations. There are no relevant studies for water polo referring to the differences presented as to the anthropometric, performance related, physiological and technical characteristics affected by training for female water polo players. The purpose of this study was to determine which of the above characteristics make athletes of the senior women's national team differ from those of the junior women's national team. The two samples of the present study were composed, respectively, of 13 athletes of the women's national team with 9.8 ± 3 years of training experience in the 26.3 ± 4.4 age group (2nd position in the Athens Olympics of 2004) and 13 athletes of the junior women's national team with 6.5 ± 1.7 years of training experience in the 17 ± 1.2 age group (4th position in the Junior European Championship of 2005). Senior female water polo players didn't differ in basic anthropometric variables when compared to the junior female players but only in limited variables. While considerably, they differed more in VO2max (50.3 ± 4.5 vs 45.3 ± 6.8 ml·kg-1·min-1), in performance in 400 m free swimming (5:24 ± 0:16 vs 5:36 ± 0:12 min:sec), in maximal lactate accumulation (8.4 ± 0.7 vs 6.4 ± 1.8 mmol·l-1), in performance in 25 free swimming (13.8 ± 0.4 vs 14.7 ± 0.8 sec), in overhead throwing velocity (16.0 ± 0.6 vs 15.1 ± 0.5 m·s-1) and on

32

water vertical jump (62.0 ± 2.7 *vs* 59.3 ± 3.0 cm), probably due to more intense and more specialized training.

Singh et al. (2008) explored that the difference in selected anthropometric and fitness variables in basketball players of selected age groups. The subjects were divided into 16 year, 17 year, and 18 years of age group. In addition to height and weight measurements, standing broad jump, standing vertical jump, 20 meter run, 6 X 10 meter shuttle run and 1500 meter run fitness tests were used to collect data. ANOVA was applied to find out the difference among selected groups and post hoc test was applied to determine the paired mean difference in case the 'F' ratio was found significant. A difference, in mean value, has been found in adjacent age groups. A significant difference in height and weight variables and a non-significant difference among selected groups. In fitness variables, have been observed.

Kong et al. (2008) conducted a study to find out the biomechanical approach to understand the success of Kenyan distance runners. Anthropometric, gait and lower extremity strength characteristics of six elite Kenyan distance runners were analyzed. Stride frequency, relative stride length and ground contact time were measured at five running speeds (3.5 – 5.4 m/s) using a motion capture system. Isometric knee extension and flexion torques were measured at six angles and hamstrings and quadriceps (H: Q) ratios at three angular velocities were determined using an isokinetic dynamometer. These runners were characterized by a low body mass index (20.1 ± 1.8 kg·m-2), low percentage body fat (5.1 ± 1.6%) and small calf circumference (34.5 ± 2.3 cm). At all running speeds, the ground contact time was shorter ($p < 0.05$) during right (170 – 212 ms) compared to left (177 – 220 ms) foot contacts. No bilateral difference was observed in other gait or strength variables. Their maximal isometric strength was lower than other runners (knee extension: 1.4 - 2.6 Nm·kg-1, knee flexion: 1.0 – 1.4 Nm·kg-1) but their H:Q ratios were higher than athletes in other sports (1.03 ± 0.51 at 60°/s, 1.44 ± 0.46 at 120°/s, 1.59 ± 0.66 at 180°/s). Further investigations are needed to confirm whether the bilateral symmetry in strength and high H: Q ratios are related to genetics, training or the lack of injuries in these runners.

Clark et al. (2008) carried out a study to examine season-to-season variations in physiological fitness parameters among a 1st team squad of professional adult male soccer players for the confirmatory purposes of identifying normative responses (immediately prior to pre-season training (PPS), mid-season (MID), and end-of-season (EOS)). Test-retest data were collected from a student population on the primary dependent variables of anaerobic threshold (AT) and maximal aerobic power (VO$_2$ max) to define meaningful measurement change in excess of test-retest technical error between test-to-test performances. In summary, despite some personnel changes in the elite cohort between test-to-test occasions, VO$_2$ max values did not vary significantly over the study which supports previous short-term observations suggesting a general 'elite' threshold of 60 ml·kg$^{-1}$ min. Interestingly, AT significantly varied where VO$_2$ max was stable and these variations also coincided with on- and off-seasons suggesting that AT is a better indication of acute training state than VO$_2$ max.

Knowles et al. (2008) examined a study to investigate the influence of maturation on physical self-perceptions and the relationship with physical activity in early adolescent girls (N = 150; mean age = 12.79 ± 0.31). Physical characteristics were measured and participants completed the physical Activity Questionnaire for Children, the Children and Youth physical Self-Perception Profile and the Pubertal Development Scale on two occasions 12 months apart. The results demonstrated a decrease in overall physical activity levels over 12 months which was not influenced by maturational status or physical characteristics. Additional analysis indicated that physical self-perceptions partially accounted for the explained variance in physical activity change, with physical condition being an important individual predictor of physical activity. Further analysis indicated that body mass was an important individual predictor of changes in perceptions of body attractiveness and physical self-worth.

Gabbett et al. (2007) conducted a study to investigate the physical performance, anthropometric, and skill characteristics of specific playing positions in sub-elite rugby league players Ninety-eight sub-elite rugby league players (mean ± S.D. age, 22.5 ± 4.9 years) participated in this study. Players underwent measurements of anthropometry (height, body mass, and sum of four skin folds), muscular power (vertical jump), speed (10 m, 20 m, and 40 m sprint), change of direction speed (L run), and maximal aerobic power (multistage fitness test). In addition, two expert coaches independently assessed the skill o f players using standardized technical criteria. Hit-up forwards were heavier and had greater skin fold thickness than the adjustable and outside backs positional groups. Furthermore, hit-up forwards had significantly ($p < 0.05$) slower change of direction speed than outside backs, and slower 20 m and 40 m speed than both the adjustable and outside backs positional groups. Hit-up forwards had a significantly greater ($p < 0.05$) ability to 'hit and spin' than both adjustable and outside backs. These findings demonstrate that the physical performance, anthropometric, and skill qualities of sub-elite rugby league players vary according to playing position.

Clare and Colin (2006) study on a squad of Premiership soccer players (n=24) provided informed consent to participate in this study. Using ISAK (International Society of Advancement of Kinanthropometry) accredited methods, a total of 39 measurements (sectioned as: skinfolds, girths, lengths, and breadths) were made for each player. The procedure involved three measures at each site to calculate a mean value and an acceptable technical error margin. All data collection was performed by an ISAK level 3 accredited anthropometrist. The data analysis consisted of demographic and anthropometric data, including fractionation of body mass and estimated body fat from sum of skinfolds. Scaling of the raw data was done by using the phantom strategem to obtain calculated data for inter-player comparison. Mean calculated scores for playing position were obtained. A multivariate analysis of variance revealed no differences between positions (F 15,41.810=0.783, P=0.688). Previous studies have reported heterogeneity between playing positions. However, in this study, stature and body mass were not different between strikers, midfielders, defenders, and goalkeepers Research has suggested that a soccer player's anthropometric dimensions can be a major determinant for success within a playing position. In this study, within-position variation was quite large in some cases, which could indicate that a team that does not have the opportunity to hand-pick players, based on anthropometric characteristics, may be at a disadvantage.

Khanna et al. (2006) carried out study to assess the morphological, physiological and biochemical characteristics of Indian National boxers as well as to assess the

35

cardiovascular adaptation to graded exercise and actual boxing round. Two different studies were conducted. In the first study [N = 60,(junior boxers below-19 yrs, n = 30), (senior boxers-20-25 yrs, n = 30)] different morphological, physiological and biochemical parameters were measured. In the second study (N = 21, Light Weight category- <54 kg, n = 7; Medium weight category <64 kg, n = 7 and Medium heavy weight category <75 kg, n = 7) cardiovascular responses were studied during graded exercise protocol and actual boxing bouts. Results showed a significantly higher (p < 0.05) stature, body mass, LBM, body fat and strength of back and grip in senior boxers compared to juniors. Significantly higher maximum heart rates were noted during actual boxing compared to graded exercise.

Young et al. (2006) carried out a study to determine the relationships between selected anthropometric and fitness measures with indicators of performance in elite junior Australian football player. During the pre-season, 485 player from the elite Victorian under-18 Australian Rules football competition were tested for height, body mass, hand span, arm length, standing reach, vertical jump, 5 and 20 m sprint times, agility, predicted $\dot{V}O_{2\,max}$ and sit and reach flexibility. The player from the top four teams had a significantly greater standing reach (p = 0.038, ES = 0.53), were heavier (p = 0.032, ES = 0.55) but not superior in any fitness measure. The small relationships between agility and flexibility to performance might be explained by the choice of tests used to assess these qualities.

Kaur et al. (2006) conducted a study to find out the various anthropometric parameter of the senior national player according to the different field positions at which they play. For this the data were collected during 54 senior nati0nal basketball championship, held at Cuttack (Orissa). The data of the 60 playing five senior basketball players of 14 reputed teams including 1st eight teams who were qualified for the national game here. The results studies have been compared with same players of foreign countries.

Schick (2006) studied to compare the physiological characteristics of amateur MMA fighters with other combat sports. Eleven male MMA fighters (age 25.5 ± 5.7y, height 174.8 ± 5.3cm, body mass 77.4 ± 11.4kg) were measured for body composition, vertical jump, flexibility, grip strength, maximal oxygen consumption

(|O2max), and relative one repetition-maximum bench press and squat. Results indicated that MMA fighters had similar body fat percentage (11.7 ± 4.0%) to judokas (11.4 ± 8.4%), but greater than wrestlers (7.6 ± 3.4%) and kung fu (9.5 ± 6.3%). Their |O2max (55.5 ± 7.3 ml/kg/min) was comparable to wrestlers (54.6 ± 2.0 ml/kg/min), but greater than judokas (48.3 ± 8.1 ml/kg/min) and less than kickboxers (62.7 ± 3.6 ml/kg/min). MMA fighters were less flexible (30.3 ± 10.6 cm) than kung fu athletes (45.5 ± 6.1 cm) but were as flexible as wrestlers (30.8 ± 5.8 cm). MMA fighters (57.6 ± 7.3 cm) had less vertical jump than wrestlers (60.0 ± 10.0 cm), both of whom were greater than kung fu (45.5 ± 6.1 cm). MMA fighters had similar relative bench press (1.2 ± 0.1 kg/kg) and relative squat (1.4 ± 0.1 kg/kg) compared to judokas (bench press 1.2 ± 0.1 kg/kg and squat 1.4 ± 0.1 kg/kg). Boxers had greater right grip strength (58.2 ± 6.9 kg) than MMA fighters (45.8 ± 6.2 kg). In conclusion, amateur MMA fighters have a physiological profile similar to judokas and wrestlers.

Pyne et al. (2006) evaluate the utility of fitness assessment and trends in drafting of players in the Australian Football League, we analyzed height, mass, skin folds, 20-m sprint, vertical jump, agility run and endurance assessed in the 495 players attending the annual national draft camps between 1999 and 2004. Effects of player's position and assessment year were expressed as standardized mean differences (Cohen effect sizes) and interpreted qualitatively. Effect of birth month on chance of being drafted, which may be important in team sports, was also analyzed. Compared with midfield players Rickman, tall forwards and tall defenders were decisively taller (effect-size range 1.33–1.95, large) and heavier (1.30–1.63, large), but had poorer sprint speed (0.23–0.57, small), aerobic ability (0.66–1.18, moderate) and agility (0.64–1.11, moderate). We conclude that fitness assessment is useful for differentiating between players positions and identifying some annual trends in recruitment in Australian football, and that players with a second half birth month have been disadvantaged with lower representation at the national draft camp.

Kumar and Kang (2006) presented a study to identify the physical fitness and its components which differentiate the champion and non-champion boxers. The investigator used Malhotra's et al.(1982) Physical fitness test . Scores on the parameters referred to above were of 24 male boxers, 12 champion boxers and 12 non-champion boxers. Quantified data which were converted into standard scores of physical fitness scores have been recorded in Tables. Further the data were statistically analyzed. Mostly men, medians, modes, standard deviations and standard errors were calculated. To test the significance of the differences between groups mean 't' ratio test was applied. The .05 and .01 levels of significance were established as the critical ratio value for the comparison.

Khanna and Manna (2006) conducted a study to the morphological, physiological and biochemical characteristics of Indian National boxers as well as to assess the cardiovascular adaptation to graded exercise and actual boxing round. Two different studies were conducted. In the first study [N = 60, (junior boxers below-19 yrs, n = 30), (senior boxers-20-25 yrs, n = 30)] different morphological, physiological and biochemical parameters were measured. In the second study (N = 21, Light Weight category- <54 kg, n = 7; Medium weight category <64 kg, n = 7 and Medium heavy weight category <75 kg, n = 7) cardiovascular responses were studied during graded exercise protocol and actual boxing bouts. Results showed a significantly higher (p < 0.05) stature, body mass, LBM, body fat and strength of back and grip in senior boxers compared to juniors. Moreover, the senior boxers possessed mesomorphic body conformation where as the juniors' possessed ectomorphic body conformation. Significantly lower (p < 0.05) aerobic capacity and anaerobic power were noted in junior boxers compared to seniors. Further, significantly higher (p < 0.05) maximal heart rates and recovery heart rates were observed in the seniors as compared to the juniors. Significantly higher maximum heart rates were noted during actual boxing compared to graded exercise. Blood lactate concentration was found to increase with the increase of workload during both graded exercise and actual boxing round. The senior boxers showed a significantly elevated (p < 0.05) levels of haemoglobin, blood urea, uric acid and peak lactate as compared to junior boxers. In the senior boxers significantly lower levels of total cholesterol, triglyceride and LDLC were observed as compared to junior boxers. No significant change has been noted in HDLC between the groups. The age and level of training in boxing has significant effect on Aerobic, anaerobic component. The study of physiological responses during graded exercise testing may be helpful to observe the cardiovascular adaptation in boxers.

Justin Keogh. (2005) conducted a study to determine if anthropometric and fitness testing scores can be used to discriminate between player that were selected or not selected in an elite Under 18 Australian Rules Football side. A training squad of 40 Australian Rules football players was assessed on a battery of standard anthropometric and fitness tests just prior to the selection of the 30 man player roster for the upcoming season. Results showed that the selected player were significantly (P < 0.05) taller and had greater upper body strength than non-selected player. This suggested that physical conditioning and anthropometric measurements do play an important part in determining selection in elite junior Australian Rules football teams.

Duncan, Woodfield and Nakeeb (2006) investigated the anthropometric and physiological characteristics of junior elite volleyball players. Twenty five national level volleyball players (mean (SD) age 17.5 (0.5) years) were assessed on a number of physiological and anthropometric variables. Somatotype was assessed using the Heath-Carter method, body composition (% body fat, % muscle mass) was assessed using surface anthropometry, leg strength was assessed using a leg and back dynamometer, low back and hamstring flexibility was assessed using the sit and reach test, and the vertical jump was used as a measure of lower body power. Maximal oxygen uptake was predicted using the 20 m multistage fitness test. Setters were more ectomorphic (p<0.05) and less mesomorphic (p<0.01) than centres. Mean (SD) of somatotype (endomorphy, mesomorphy, ectomorphy) for setters and centres was 2.6 (0.9), 1.9 (1.1), 5.3 (1.2) and 2.2 (0.8), 3.9 (1.1), 3.6 (0.7) respectively. Hitters had significantly greater low back and hamstring flexibility than opposites. Mean (SD) for sit and reach was 19.3 (8.3) cm for opposites and 37 (10.7) cm for hitters. There were no other significant differences in physiological and anthropometric variables across playing positions (all p>0.05). Setters tend to be endomorphic ectomorphs, hitters and opposites tend to be balanced ectomorphs, whereas centres tend to be ectomorphic mesomorphs. These results indicate the need for sports scientists and conditioning professionals to take the body type of volleyball players into account when designing individualised position specific training programmes.

Chauhan (2003) studied to determine the relationship between anthropometric variables and the middle distance running performance and also to develop regression equation for the prediction of performance of the athletes between the age range of 18 and 30 years. The data was collected from 1500 mtrs. Middle distance runners as subjects of the study by using anthropometric, skin fold caliper, vernier caliper and steel tape. The product moment method for correlation and wherry do little method for calculating multiple correlation and development of regression equation were utilized. Linear measurements, i.e. height, leg length, thigh length, total arm length, girth measurements, i.e. shoulder, chest, abdominal, hip, thigh, and knee, body diameters, i.e. biacromial and ankle diameters, thigh (negative) and calf skin fold, lean body mass and age have positive and significant correlations with middle distance running performance. The multiple correlation of a selected combination of variables (i.e. height, thigh girth, biacromial diameter and thigh skin fold) with middle distance running performance have been found significant but the multiple correlation is not of sufficient size, so the regression equation developed cannot be put in the prediction of middle distance running performance.

Rodriguez et al. (2003) examined a study to assess the estrogenic effects of sport activities before puberty. One hundred four healthy white boys (9.3 ± 0.2 years, Tanner stages I–II) participated in this study: 53 footballers and 51 controls. The footballers devoted at least 3 h per week to participation in football, while the controls did not perform in any kind of regular physical activity other than that programmed during the compulsory physical education courses. Bone variables were measured by dual-energy X-ray absorptiometry. The maximal leg extension isometric force in the squat position with knees bent at 90° and the peak force, mean power, and height jumped during vertical jumps were assed with a force plate. Additionally, 30-m running speed, 300-m run (anaerobic capacity), and 20-m shuttle-run tests (maximal aerobic power) were also performed. Compared to the controls, the footballers attained better results in the physical fitness test and had lower body mass (−10%, P < 0.05) due to a reduced percentage of body fat (4% less, P < 0.05). The footballer's exhibit enhanced trochanteric BMC (+17%, P < 0.001). Likewise, femoral and lumbar spine BMD was also greater in the football players (P ≤ 0.05). In summary, football participation is associated with improved physical fitness reduced fat mass, increased lean body and BMC masses, and enhanced femoral and lumbar spine BMD in prepubertal boys. The combination of anthropometric and fitness variables may be useful to detect children with potentially reduced bone mass.

Rodriguez et al. (2002) evaluated the effect of physical activity on the bone content (BMC) and density (BMD) in 51 girls (14.2 ± 0.4 yr). Twenty-four were placed in the handball group as they have been playing handball for at least 1 year

(3.9 ± 0.4). The other 27 who did not perform in any kind of regular physical activity other than that programmed during the compulsory physical education courses comprised the control group. Bone mass and areal density was measured by dual-energy X-ray absorptiometry (DXA). The maximal leg extension isometric force in the squat position with knees bent at 90° and the peak force, mean power, and height jumped during vertical squat jump were assessed with a force plate. Additionally, 30-m run (running speed) and 300-m run (as an estimate of anaerobic capacity) tests were also performed. Maximal aerobic capacity was estimated using the 20-m shuttle-run tests. Compared to the controls, hand ballers attained better results in the physical fitness tests and had a 6% and 11% higher total body and right upper extremity lean mass (all P < 0.05). The hand ballers showed enhanced BMC and BMD in the lumbar spine, pelvic region, and lower extremity (all P < 0.05). In conclusion, handball participation is associated with improved physical fitness increased lean and bone masses, and enhanced axial and appendicle BMD in young girls.

Rodriguez et al. (2002) evaluated the effect of physical activity on the bone content (BMC) and density (BMD) in 51 girls (14.2 ± 0.4 yr). Twenty-four were placed in the handball group as they have been playing handball for at least 1 year (3.9 ± 0.4). The other 27 who did not perform in any kind of regular physical activity other than that programmed during the compulsory physical education courses comprised the control group. Bone mass and areal density was measured by dual-energy X-ray absorptiometry (DXA). The maximal leg extension isometric force in the squat position with knees bent at 90° and the peak force, mean power, and height jumped during vertical squat jump were assessed with a force plate. Additionally, 30-m run (running speed) and 300-m run (as an estimate of anaerobic capacity) tests were also performed. Maximal aerobic capacity was estimated using the 20-m shuttle-run tests. In conclusion, handball participation is associated with improved physical fitness increased lean and bone masses, and enhanced axial and appendicle BMD in young girls. The combination of anthropometric and fitness related variables may be used to detect girls with potentially reduced bone mass.

Kaur et al. (2001) revealed that the highlights of anthropometric and fitness profile of Asian gold medallists Indian male kabaddi players. Various linear body measurements, circumferences, skin folds thicknesses along with few physical performance test viz. standing broad jump, pull ups, 30 m run, 6 X 10 m shuttle run and 2.4 km. run were taken by using standard techniques. The present kabaddi players ranged in age from 20 to 34 year and are 175.26 cm tell and 76.67 kg heavy. The value of bony diameters indicates that they well developed mass in the body due to bones (17.87 kg). the different circumferential measurements though founds in good range, have given 34.39 kg muscle mass in their body which needs further improvement. The per cent body fat 17.14 % which is towards higher side and need to be reduced the level of below 14 % somatotype ratings (2.67-5.46-1.97) highlight the need for further improvements in the development of muscles. Height-weight ratio also indicates that the players are overweight with respect to height. Follow up testing of physical fitness variables have indicated overall improvement in their fitness. Significant improvements has been noticed in pull ups, 2.4 kg run and 6 X 20 m shuttle run at the end of the training camp. Perhaps, this is the best time to highlight other scientific discrepancies also if any, so that the same can be rectified for the excellent performance in coming 2002 Asian Games.

Glazier et al. (2000) examined a study to find out significant relationships between selected anthropometric and kinematic variables and ball release speed. Nine collegiate fast-medium bowlers (mean ± s: age $21.0 \pm 0.9$ years, body mass $77.2 \pm 8.1$ kg, height $1.83 \pm 0.1$ m) were reconstructed three-dimensionally. Ball release speeds were measured by a previously validated Speed check TM Personal Sports Radar (Tribar Industries, Canada). Relationships between selected anthropometric variables and ball release speed and between kinematic variables and ball release speed were investigated using Pearson's product± moment correlation coeý cients (r). A sign cant relationship was found between the horizontal velocity during the pre-delivery stride ($r = 0.728$, $P < 0.05$) and ball release speed ($31.5 \pm 1.9$ m′ s- 1). We believe that the high correlation was due to the bowlers using techniques that allowed them to contribute more of the horizontal velocity created during the run-up to ball release speed. We also found that the angular velocity ($40.6 \pm 3.4$ rad ′ s- 1) of the right humerus had a low correlation ($r = 0.358$, $P > 0.05$) with ball release speed. Although the action of the wrist was not analysed because of an inadequate frame rate, we found high correlations between ball release speed and shoulder± wrist length ($661 \pm 31$ mm; $r = 0.626$, $P < 0.05$) and ball release speed and total arm length ($860 \pm 36$

mm; r = 0.583, P < 0.05). He concludes that the variance in release speed within this group may be accounted for by the diþerence in radial length between the axis of rotation at the glen humeral joint and the release point.

Kemper et al. (2000) assessed the effects of physical activity are often reported, there are still uncertainties about the type, intensity, duration, and frequency of these activities that are most effective for (re)modeling bone mass during youth. In the Amsterdam Growth and Health Longitudinal Study, daily physical activity and fitness were monitored from age 13 to 29 years in a group of 182 males and females. At a mean age of 28 years, bone mineral density (BMD) was measured at three sites with dual X-ray absorptiometry (DXA): in the lumbar region (lumbar BMD), the femoral neck (hip BMD), and the distal radius (wrist BMD). physical activity (PA) was estimated from a cross-check activity interview taking in consideration all daily physical activities during the last 3 months; PA was scored in two different ways: (1) metabolic physical activity score (METPA) by weighting the intensity (multiples of basic metabolic rate [METs]) and duration (minutes per week); and (2) mechanic physical activity score (MECHPA) by weighting the peak strain (ground reaction forces as multiples of body mass) irrespective of frequency and duration of the physical activities. Physical fitness was measured with a neuromoter fitness test (composite of six strength, flexibility, and speed tests) and as cardiopulmonary fitness (maximal oxygen uptake). This was not the case for cardio respiratory fitness. No significant correlations at all are found with wrist BMD, a bone site that is less involved in physical activity and fitness  It can be concluded that daily physical activity during adolescence and in the young adult period is significantly related to the BMD at the lumbar spine and femoral neck at age 28 of males and females. Only neuromoter fitness and not cardiopulmonary fitness during adolescence and young adulthood is related to the BMD of males and females at age 28 years.

Gabbett (2000) investigated the physiological and anthropometric characteristics of amateur rugby league players. Thirty five amateur rugby league players (19 forwards and 16 backs) were measured for height, body mass, percentage body fat (sum of four skinfolds), muscular power (vertical jump), speed (10 m and 40 m sprint), and maximal aerobic power (multistage fitness test). Data were also collected on match frequency, training status, playing experience, and employment related physical activity levels. The 10 m and 40 m sprint, vertical jump, percentage body fat, and multistage fitness test results were 20–42% poorer than previously reported for professional rugby league players. Compared with forwards, backs had significantly (p<0.01) lower body mass (79.7 (74.7–84.7) kg $v$ 90.8 (86.2–95.4) kg) and significantly (p<0.01) greater speed during the 40 m sprint (6.45 (6.35–6.55) $v$ 6.79 (6.69–6.89) seconds). Values for percentage body fat, vertical jump, 10 m sprint, and maximal aerobic power were not significantly different (p>0.05) between forwards and backs. When compared with professional rugby league players, the training status of amateur rugby league players was 30–53% lower, with players devoting less than three hours a week to team training sessions and about 30 minutes a week to individual training sessions. The training time devoted to the development of muscular power (about 13 minutes a week), speed (about eight minutes a week), and aerobic fitness (about 34 minutes a week) did not differ significantly (p>0.05) between forwards and backs. At the time of the field testing, players had participated, on average, in one 60 minute match every eight days. The physiological and anthropometric characteristics of amateur rugby league players are poorly developed. These findings suggest that position specific training does not occur in amateur rugby league. The poor fitness of non-elite players may be due to a low playing intensity, infrequent matches of short duration, and/or an inappropriate training stimulus.

Randy and Peter (1995) investigated the anthropometric and physiological characteristics of kick boxers. Professional male middleweight (73-77 kg) and welterweight (63-67 kg) kick boxers were determined to have relatively higher aerobic capacities ([latin capital V with dot above]O2max, 54-69 ml [middle dot] kg-1 [middle dot] min-1), anaerobic capacities (8.2-11.2 W [middle dot] kg-1), and knee extension peak torques (2.8-3.3 Nm [middle dot] kg-1 @ 60[degrees] [middle dot] sec-1) than previously reported for many other power or combat athletes. Kickboxers also tended to be lean (6.1-10.8% BF) and were classified as mesomedial body types on the Health-Carter somatotype scale. This suggests that elite kickboxers demonstrate a high level of aerobic and anaerobic conditioning along with the ability to produce high muscle forces.

Frank and Robert (1985) conducted a study to find out the physical fitness superiority of athletes over no athlete's increases as a function of age, the magnitude of athlete-nonathletic fitness differences are the same in males as in females, and these differences are consistent across ages. Approximately 3,000 students in grades 3, 7, and 11 (ages 9, 13, and 17 years) were tested on measures of static and explosive muscular strength, static and dynamic muscular endurance, cardiovascular endurance, and flexibility. ANOVA and follow-up univariate ANOVAs indicated that the higher the grade, the better the performance; males outperformed females on all measures except flexibility; and athletes were superior to non athletes on all six test items. Furthermore, (a) there was no difference between athletes and non athletes at grade 3, athletes were considerably better than non-athletes by grade 7, and the magnitude of the difference was virtually the same at grade 11, (b) the fitness superiority of athletes over non-athletes was essentially of the same magnitude for males as for females at each grade level.

Maud (1983) study to describe the anthropometric and physiological parameters that apply to a USA amateur rugby union club team. Fifteen players who were members of the club's first team were evaluated for body composition, muscular strength, power and endurance, flexibility, anaerobic power, anaerobic capacity, and cardio-respiratory function shortly after completion of the regular season. Means for some of the variables measured include: age, 29 yr; height, 180 cm; weight, 84 kg; lean body weight, 74 kg; body fat, 12%, endurance sit-ups, 50/min; vertical jump height, 51 cm; anaerobic power output, 132 m.kg.s-1 (1.32 kw); anaerobic capacity, 2247 m.kp/40s (22.5 kJ); maximum heart rate, 186 beats/min; maximum ventilation, 175 l/min-1; maximum respiratory quotient 1.23; and maximum oxygen uptake, 56.6 ml.kg-1 min-1. In comparison with other rugby players studied these players had higher maximum oxygen uptake values, were similar in endurance sit-up and vertical jump ability, exhibited less upper body strength, and the forwards had lower body fat percentages. They were generally within the range of scores found to describe the aerobic and anaerobic fitness, and body composition of other élite amateur and professional intermittent sport athletes.

## Chapter - III

# Research Design and Methodology

## Introduction

*This chapter describes the research design and specific methodology to be adopted. The purpose of the study was to find out the difference of Physical, Physiological and Anthropometric Characteristics of Punjab and Haryana Boxers. The purpose of this chapter is to describe the methodologies employed and their application. The chapter is organized in sections covering:*

i. *Selection of Subjects*

ii. *Selection of Variables*

iii. *Administration of Test*

iv. *Design of the Study*

v. *Statistical Techniques Employed*

# SELECTION OF SUBJECTS

For the purpose of the present study, One Hundred Sixty (N=160) subjects between the age group of 19-28 years were selected. The subjects were purposively assigned into two groups: Group-A: Punjab Boxers ($N_1$=80) and Group-B: Haryana Boxers ($N_2$=80). All the subjects were informed about the objective and protocol of the study.

# SELECTION OF VARIABLES

A feasibility analysis as to which of the variables could be taken up for the investigation, keeping in view the availability of tools, adequacy to the subjects and the legitimate time that could be devoted for tests and to keep the entire study unitary and integrated was made in consultation with experts. With the above criteria's in mind, the following variables were selected for the present study:

I.   Physical Fitness Components:
    i.   Speed
    ii.   Agility
    iii.   Balance
    iv.   Coordination
    v.   Reaction Time
    vi.   Power

II.   Physiological Characteristics:
    i.   Vital Capacity
    ii.   Resting Pulse Rate
    iii.   Peak Flow Rate

III.   Anthropometric Characteristics:
  i.   Standing height
  ii.   Body weight
  iii.   Leg length
  iv.   Upper leg length
  v.   Lower leg length
  vi.   Arm length
  vii.   Upper arm length
  viii.   Lower arm length
  ix.   Hip width (bitrochantric diameter)

x.      Shoulder width (biacromial diameter)

xi.     Chest width

xii.    Calf girth

xiii.   Thigh girth

xiv.    Chest girth

xv.     Upper arm girth

xvi.    Lower arm girth

# ADMINISTRATION OF TEST

**Physical Fitness Components:**

## SPEED

**(20 Meter Dash)**

- **Purpose:** To measure acceleration, and also a reliable indicator of speed, agility and quickness.
- **Equipment required:** Measuring Tape or marked track, stopwatch or timing gates, cone markers, flat and clear surface of at least 40 meters.
- **Procedure:** The test involves running a single maximum sprint over 20 meters, with the time recorded. A thorough warm up should be given, including some practice starts and accelerations. Start from a stationary position, with one foot in front of the other. The front foot must be on or behind the starting line. This starting position should be held for 2 seconds prior to starting, and no rocking movements are allowed. The tester should provide hints to maximizing speed (such as keeping low, driving hard with the arms and legs) and encouraged to continue running hard past the finish line.
- **Scoring:** Two trials are allowed, and the best time is recorded to the nearest 2 decimal places. The timing starts from the first movement and finishes when the chest crosses the finish line.

## AGILITY

**(Illinois Agility Test)**

- **Purpose:** To test running agility
- **Equipment required:** Flat non-slip surface, marking cones, stopwatch, measuring tape, timing gates (optional)
- **Procedure:** The length of the course is 10 meters and the width (distance between the start and finish points) is 5 meters. Four cones are used to mark

the start, finish and the two turning points. Another four cones are placed down the center an equal distance apart. Each cone in the center is spaced 3.3 meters apart. Subjects should lie on their front (head to the start line) and hands by their shoulders. On the 'Go' command the stopwatch is started, and the athlete gets up as quickly as possible and runs around the course in the direction indicated, without knocking the cones over, to the finish line, at which the timing is stopped.

- **Scoring:** Two or more trails may be performed, and the quickest time is recorded.

## BALANCE

### (Stork Balance Stand Test)

- **Purpose**: To assess the ability to balance on the ball of the foot.
- **Equipment required:** Flat, non-slip surface, stopwatch, paper and pencil.
- **Procedure:** Remove the shoes and place the hands on the hips, then position the non-supporting foot against the inside knee of the supporting leg. The subject is given one minute to practice the balance. The subject raises the heel to balance on the ball of the foot. The stopwatch is started as the heel is raised from the floor. The stopwatch is stopped if any of the follow occurs:
  o The hand(s) come off the hips .
  o The supporting foot swivels or moves (hops) in any direction.
  o The non-supporting foot loses contact with the knee.
  o The heel of the supporting foot touches the floor.

Scoring: The total time in seconds is recorded. The score is the best of three attempts

## COORDINATION

### (Eye Hand Coordination Test)

- **Purpose:** To test the coordination between eyes hands.
- **Equipment Required:** Two large boxes or containers (capable of holding more than 5 balls of 10 inches diameter each) and a stopwatch.
- **Procedure:** The tester after giving a demonstration, asked the subject to stand in the middle of two boxes which lay at a distance of 15 feet from each other. Five or more ordinary playground balls of 10" diameter were put in the box lying on the left hand side of the subject. The tester gave the commands ready, steady, go! At the word go, the tester switched on the stopwatch while the subject ran to the box on his left, took out one ball, ran to the right box, put the

ball in the box, ran back to the left box to take another ball for putting in the right box and repeated the process till the last ball was put in the right box. As soon as the subject put the last ball in the right box, the tester stopped the stopwatch to record the time taken by the subject to transfer all the five or more (up to 10 balls, if the tester wants to, measure co-ordination, agility and speed simultaneously).

- **Scoring:** The subject was given two trials after a slow practice trail. The best timing was the score of the test. However a variety of scoring was used by the tester's depending upon the variety of ways the ball transfer skill has been tested by the physical educators and coaches. Accordingly, scoring was, correct number of balls transferred (during distance tossing), number of complete correct trails out of given number of trails or the time taken to perform the specified job.

## REACTION TIME

### (Ball Reaction Exercise Test)

- **Purpose:** This test was administered to measure the reaction ability of the subjects.
- **Equipment required:** Two wooden planks each of 4 cm. length, one inflated volleyball, a supporting stand Pencil, papers & Pad
- **Procedure:** Two wooden planks of four meters each were kept in a lined by a supporting stand having a height of one meter and twenty centimeters. So that it could enable volleyball to roll freely from a height of 1.20 m. The lower ends of the planks were graduated in centimeters. Volleyball was held by the tester at the top of the planks. The subject was asked to stand behind the starting line, facing opposite to the planks on clapping. The subject took a turn and run towards the planks which was dropped on the ball width both the hands which was dropped on the signal each subject was given a practice trial before actual commencement of the test.
- **Scoring:** The soccer was the distance measured in cms. from the top of the planks to a point where the subject stopped the ball, only two trials were given and the best one was recorded as the score of the subject.

## POWER

### (Vertical Jump Test)

- **Purpose:** To measure the power of legs in jumping vertically

- **Equipment required:** Measuring Tape or marked wall, chalk for marking wall or jump mat.
- **Procedure:** The athlete stands side on to a wall and reaches up with the hand closest to the wall. Keeping the feet flat on the ground, the point of the fingertips is marked or recorded. This is called the standing reach height. The athlete then stands away from the wall, and leaps vertically as high as possible using both arms and legs to assist in projecting the body upwards. The jumping technique can or cannot use a countermovement (see vertical jump technique). Attempt to touch the wall at the highest point of the jump. The difference in distance between the standing reach height and the jump height is the score. The best of three attempts is recorded.
- **Scoring:** The jump height is usually recorded as a distance score.

**Physiological Characteristics:**

The following Physiological Characteristics were measured 3 times, the respective average values being used in the analysis:

## VITAL CAPACITY (VC)

- The vital capacity (VC) was the volume, measured at the mouth, between the position of full inspiration and expiration. It was the total amount of air that an individual can breathe in and out of their lungs in a single maximum breath. Vital capacity was measured by a spirometer. Spirometer was calibrated to record the true volume of air exhaled into or through them. The accuracy of this calibration was checked with a calibration syringe to ensure that the spirometer continues to record volumes accurately. The subject was made to sit and breathe normally through the mouthpiece of spirometer. It was made sure the nose clips were on. Subjects filled their lung as much as possible. As soon as they had their lungs fully inflated, they blew all the air out as fast as they could. Then mouthpieces were removed. Nose clips were taken off. The best of 3 Forced Vital Capacity (FVC) manoeuvres were taken.

## RESTING PULSE RATE

- Heart rate was measured by finding the pulse of the body. This pulse rate can be measured at any point on the body where an artery's pulsation is transmitted to the surface - often as it is compressed against an underlying structure like bone - by pressuring it with the index and middle finger. The thumb should not be used for measuring another person's heart rate, as its

51

strong pulse may interfere with discriminating the site of pulsation or use stethoscope or electronic automatic machine for exact calculation of the beats. The beats per minute were usually recorded as score.

## PEAK FLOW RATE

- Expiratory peak flow (PEF) was the maximum flow generated during expiration performed with maximal force and started after a full inspiration. The subject was made to stand up and it was ensured that the indicator was at the bottom of the meter (zero). The subject was then asked to take a deep breath in, filling the lungs completely and place the mouthpiece in the mouth; lightly bite with the teeth and close the lips on it. The subject was asked to keep the tongue away from the mouthpiece and blast the air out as hard and as fast as possible in a single blow. The best of three readings was used as the recorded value of the peak expiratory flow rate.

**Anthropometric Characteristics:**

## STANDING HEIGHT

- **Purpose:** To measure the height of the subjects.
- **Equipment required:** Stadiometer.
- **Procedure:** The subject was asked to stand erect, bare footed on a plane horizontal surface against a wall with his heel, back of the shoulder and head touching the wall. He was asked to stretch the body upwards as much as possible without his heels leaving the ground. The head and face was checked for its being in frontal horizontal plane. To get it easily, the subject was asked to see towards an object in front of him approximately at a height of his eyes, and then the investigator adjusts the tracheon and infraorbitale points in a horizontal line. The anthropometer rod was kept in front of the subject and the cross bar of the anthropometer were adjusted so that its lower edge touches the highest point of the subject's head (i.e. point vertex). The measurement was recorded from the anthropmeters eye correct up to 0.1cm.

## WEIGHT

- **Purpose:** To measure the weight of the subjects.
- **Equipment required:** Weighing machine.
- **Procedure:** The measurement were taken in a laboratory, lever balanced is preferred. The subject was asked to take off his shoes and clothes except brief

and under garments. The subject stands erect on the platform and balance with equal weight on both feet. The weight was recorded accurate up to 0.01 kg.

## LEG LENGTH

- **Purpose:** To measure the leg length of the subjects.
- **Equipment required** Flexible steel tape.
- **Procedure:** Leg length was measured vertically from the bottom outside edge of the foot in the center of the instep to a line draws horizontally through the mid gluteus bulge at the point tendency to a vertical line contracting the buttocks. The tape was placed at the center of the instep and measured to tip of iliac. Leg length was recorded correct to the nearest half centimeters.

## UPPER LEG LENGTH

- **Purpose:** To measure the upper leg length of the subjects.
- **Equipment required:** Flexible steel tape.
- **Procedure:** Subject stands erect in standing position. The upper leg length was measured with the help of flexible steel tape from the distance from the iliospinale to tibiae. The upper leg length was recorded correct to the nearest half a centimeter.

## LOWER LEG LENGTH

- **Purpose:** To measure the lower leg length of the subjects.
- **Equipment required:** Flexible steel tape.
- **Procedure:** Subject stand erect with his feet placed 6 to 8 inches apart and the body weight evenly distributed on both the feet using the anthropometer, measure the distance from tibiae to the floor. The lower leg length was recorded correct to the nearest half a centimeter.

## ARM LENGTH

- **Purpose:** To measure the arm length of the subjects.
- **Equipment required:** Flexible steel tape.
- **Procedure:** Arm length was taken from the acromion process to the tip of the third finger. The arm length was measured with a flexible steel tape. It is recorded to the nearest half a centimeter.

## UPPER ARM LENGTH

- **Purpose:** To measure the upper arm length of the subjects.
- **Equipment required:** Flexible steel tape.

- **Procedure:** The subject stood erect by keeping his arms along with his body. Upper arm length was measured with the flexible steel tape. The tip of the tape was placed at the upper edge of the head of acromiale to the tip of the point of radiale. The upper arm length was recorded correct to the nearest half of a centimeter.

## LOWER ARM LENGTH

- **Purpose:** To measure the lower arm length of the subjects.
- **Equipment required:** Flexible steel tape.
- **Procedure:** The subjects were instructed to stand erects and relaxed. Fore arm length was measured with the flexible steel tape. The tip of the tape was placed at the upper edge of the head of the radius to the tip of the middle finger. The fore arm length was recorded correct to the nearest half a centimeter.

## HIP WIDTH (BITROCHANTRIC DIAMETER)

- **Purpose:** To measure the hip width of the subjects.
- **Equipment required:** Sliding calipers.
- **Procedure:** The subject was asked to stand erect with heels together and arms about six inches away from the body. The tester standing behind the subject, applies the inner sides of the sliding calipers to the left and right trochanterion points on the two femur and presses the two cross bars hard so to minimize the soft tissue width. Hip width was recorded correct to the nearest half centimeter.

## SHOULDER WIDTH (BIACROMIAL DIAMETER)

- **Purpose:** To measure the shoulder width of the subjects.
- **Equipment required:** Sliding calipers, skin marking pencil.
- **Procedure:** The subject was asked to stand erect with shoulder dropping a little forward. The investigator marks the acromiale points with a skin marking pencil. While standing at a back of the subject, the tips of the two cross-bars of the sliding calipers are made to touch the acromiale points on both the shoulders along with the tips of fore fingers of the investigator so as to ensure firm grip of compass on the outer border of the acromian process with a mild pressure. Shoulder width was recorded correct to the nearest half centimeter.

## CHEST WIDTH

- **Purpose:** To measure the chest width of the subjects.

- **Equipment required:** Sliding calipers.
- **Procedure:** The subject was asked to stand erect with heels together and arms about six inches away from the body. The investigator stands in front of the subject and applies the tips of the two cross-bar to the lateral most points (Iliocristale) of the Iliac crests pressing hard the over lying subcutaneous fat. Chest width was recorded correct to the nearest half centimeter.

## CALF GIRTH

- **Purpose:** To measure the calf girth of the subjects.
- **Equipment required:** A flexible steel tape.
- **Procedure:** The flexible steel tape was wrapped horizontally around the marked lower leg of the subject at the maximal bulge of the calf muscle with slight up and down movements of the steel tape keeping it in a horizontal direction. The maximal girth measurement gives the value of calf girth. The measurement was recorded nearest of a centimeter.

## THIGH GIRTH

- **Purpose:** To measure the thigh girth of the subjects.
- **Equipment required:** Flexible steel tape and skin marking pencil
- **Procedure:** The subject wearing only under wear was asked to stand at ease with equal weight on both the feet. The middle of the thigh was marked by a horizontal line dividing the distance between the trochanterion and the lateral and lower most point on the lateral condyle of femur, in two equal parts. The steel tape was wrapped around the thigh at the level of the horizontal line and the girth was measured by keeping the steel tape in a horizontal direction and touching gently thigh surface all around. The measurement was recorded nearest of a centimeter.

## CHEST GIRTH

- **Purpose:** To measure the chest girth of the subjects..
- **Equipment required:** Flexible steel tape and skin marking pencil.
- **Procedure:** The subject was asked to take off the clothes from his upper body. A steel tape was wrapped round his chest in such a way that it touches the body all around lightly. The tape should lie over the nipples in front and should pass just below the inferior borders of the scapulae at the back. To note the normal chest girth, the subject was asked to breath normal and the measurement is taken at the end of the normal expiration. Then the subject

were instructed to inhale as deep as possible and a maximum value was achieved from the expanded chest at the end of the best effort inspiration after a good deal of motivation. The measurement was recorded nearest of a centimeter.

### UPPER ARM GIRTH

- **Purpose:** To measure the upper arm girth of the subjects.
- **Equipment required:** Flexible steel tape and marking pencil.
- **Procedure:** The subject was asked to stand at ease with equal weight on both the feet and with hands hanging freely. The upper-arm girth was usually measured on the left naked upper arm. Locating the point's acromiale and radial the midpoint of these two points was marked with a skin marking pencil by a horizontal line. The flexible steel tape was wrapped around the upper-arm at the marked level keeping the tape horizontal and touching lightly to the skin all around. The measurement was recorded nearest of centimeter.

### LOWER ARM GIRTH

- **Purpose:** To measure the lower arm girth of the subjects.
- **Equipment required:** Flexible steel tape
- **Procedure:** The subject was asked to stand as in the case of upper-arm girth with naked forearm. The steel tape was wrapped around the fore-arm just below the elbow point and the maximal measurement were recorded by moving the steel tape slightly up and down keeping the circle of tape in horizontal direction and touching all around. The measurement was recorded nearest of a centimeter.

## DESIGN OF THE STUDY

This is an exploratory study that has employed method of data collection and analysis quantitatively.The purpose of the study was to find out the difference of Physical, Physiological and Anthropometric Characteristics of Punjab and Haryana Boxers. The purposive sampling technique was used to attain the objectives of the study.

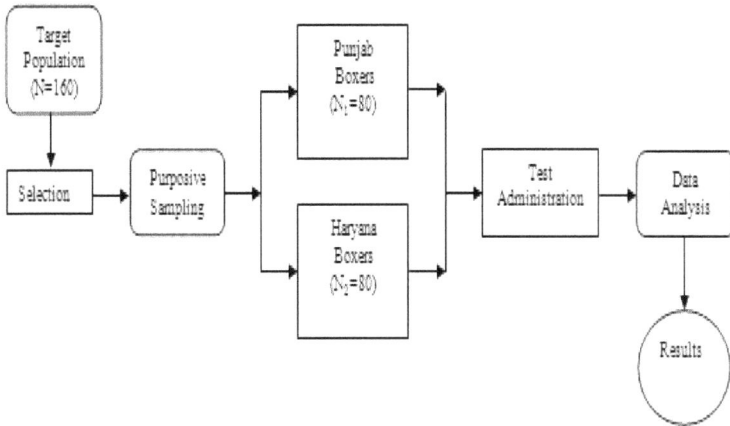

```
┌──────────────┐        ┌──────────────┐
│   Target     │        │   Punjab     │
│ Population   │        │   Boxers     │
│  (N=160)     │        │  (N₁=80)     │
└──────┬───────┘        └──────────────┘
       │
       ▼
┌──────────────┐   ┌──────────────┐
│  Selection   │──▶│  Purposive   │──▶
└──────────────┘   │  Sampling    │
                   └──────────────┘

        ┌──────────────┐
        │   Haryana    │
        │   Boxers     │
        │  (N₂=80)     │
        └──────────────┘

┌──────────────┐   ┌──────────────┐
│     Test     │──▶│     Data     │
│Administration│   │   Analysis   │
└──────────────┘   └──────────────┘
                          │
                          ▼
                      ( Results )
```

## STATISTICAL TECHNIQUE EMPLOYED

The Statistical Package for the Social Sciences (SPSS) version 14.0 was used for all analyses. The differences in the mean of each group for selected variable were tested for the significance of difference by t-test. In all the analyses, the 5% critical level ($p < 0.05$) was considered to indicate statistical significance.

## Chapter - IV

# Data Analysis and Research Findings

## Introduction

In this chapter the results of the data analysis are presented. The methodology described in the previous chapter provided the baseline for data gathering. This chapter at the outset describes the analysis of data followed research findings. Data were analysed to find out the significant difference of Physical, Physiological and Anthropometric Characteristics of Punjab and Haryana Boxers. The research findings are discussed with reference to the research problem outlined in chapter-I and the literature in chapter-II to highlight similarities and different findings.

# ANALYSIS OF DATA

This is an exploratory study that has employed methods of data collection and analysis quantitatively. The purpose of this study was to find out the significant difference of Physical, Physiological and Anthropometric Characteristics of Punjab and Haryana Boxers.
The objectives of the study were to:

1. To find out the significant difference of Physical Fitness Components (i.e., Speed, Agility, Balance, Coordination, Reaction Time and Power) among Punjab and Haryana boxers.
2. To find out the significant difference of Physiological Characteristics (i.e., Vital Capacity, Pulse Rate and Peak Flow Rate) among Punjab and Haryana boxers.
3. To find out the significant differences of Anthropometric Characteristics (i.e., Standing Height, Weight, Leg Length, Upper Leg Length, Lower Leg Length, Arm Length, Upper Arm Length, Lower Arm Length, Hip Width, Shoulder Width, Chest Width, Calf Girth, Thigh Girth, Chest Girth, Upper Arm Girth and Lower Arm Girth) among Punjab and Haryana boxers.

The researcher collected the data from One Hundred Sixty (N=160) subjects between the age group of 19-28 years were selected. The subjects were purposively assigned into two groups: Group-A: Punjab Boxers ($N_1$=80) and Group-B: Haryana Boxers ($N_2$=80). All the subjects were informed about the objective and protocol of the study.

# FINDINGS

For each of the chosen variable Physical, Physiological and Anthropometric Characteristics the result pertaining to significant difference, if any, is presented in following tables:

**Table 1: Mean Values (±SD), Standard Error of the Mean and Test Statistic t of Speed in Punjab Boxers (N = 80) and Haryana Boxers (N = 80).**

|  | Punjab Boxers | Haryana Boxers |
|---|---|---|
| Sample size | 80 | 80 |
| Arithmetic mean | 8.02 | 7.87 |
| 95% CI for the mean | 7.90 to 8.14 | 7.81 to 7.93 |
| Variance | 0.28 | 0.07 |
| Standard deviation | 0.53 | 0.27 |
| Standard error of the mean | 0.059 | 0.03 |
| Difference |  | 0.15 |
| Standard Error |  | 0.06 |
| 95% CI of difference |  | 0.28 to 0.02 |
| Test statistic t |  | 2.289 |
| Degrees of Freedom (DF) |  | 158 |
| Two-tailed probability |  | P<0.023 |

**\*Significant at 0.05 level**          **Degree of freedom= 158**

Table-1 presents the results of Punjab boxers and Haryana boxers with regard to the variable Speed. The descriptive statistics shows the Mean and SD values of Punjab boxers on the sub-variable Speed as 8.02 and 0.53 respectively. However, Haryana boxers had Mean and SD values as 7.87 and 0.27 respectively. The Mean Difference and Standard Error Difference of Mean were 0.15 and 0.06 respectively. The 't'-value 2.289 as shown in the table above was found statistically significant (P<.05). But while comparing the mean values of both the groups, it has been observed that Haryana boxers have demonstrated better Speed than the Punjab boxers. The comparison of mean scores of both the groups has been presented graphically in figure-1.

**Table 2: Mean Values (±SD), Standard Error of the Mean and Test Statistic t of Agility in Punjab Boxers (N = 80) and Haryana Boxers (N = 80).**

|  | Punjab Boxers | Haryana Boxers |
|---|---|---|
| Sample size | 80 | 80 |
| Arithmetic mean | 14.08 | 14.00 |
| 95% CI for the mean | 13.99 to 14.16 | 13.96 to 14.04 |
| Variance | 0.13 | 0.032 |
| Standard deviation | 0.37 | 0.18 |
| Standard error of the mean | 0.041 | 0.02 |
| Difference |  | 0.07 |
| Standard Error |  | 0.04 |
| 95% CI of difference |  | 0.17 to 0.012 |
| Test statistic t |  | 1.712 |
| Degrees of Freedom (DF) |  | 158 |
| Two-tailed probability |  | P >0.08 |

**\*Significant at 0.05 level**                                       **Degree of freedom= 158**

Table-2 presents the results of Punjab boxers and Haryana boxers with regard to the variable Agility. The descriptive statistics shows the Mean and SD values of Punjab boxers on the sub-variable Agility as 14.08 and 0.37 respectively. However, Haryana boxers had Mean and SD values as 14.00 and 0.18 respectively. The Mean Difference and Standard Error Difference of Mean were 0.07 and 0.04 respectively. The 't'-value 1.712 as shown in the table above was found statistically insignificant (P>.05). But while comparing the mean values of both the groups, it has been observed that Haryana boxers have demonstrated better Agility than the Punjab boxers. The comparison of mean scores of both the groups has been presented graphically in figure-2.

**Table 3: Mean Values (±SD), Standard Error of the Mean and Test Statistic t of Balance in Punjab Boxers (N = 80) and Haryana Boxers (N = 80).**

|  | Punjab Boxers | Haryana Boxers |
|---|---|---|
| Sample size | 80 | 80 |
| Arithmetic mean | 26.70 | 29.00 |
| 95% CI for the mean | 25.35 to 28.04 | 27.42 to 30.57 |
| Variance | 36.36 | 49.97 |
| Standard deviation | 6.03 | 7.06 |
| Standard error of the mean | 0.67 | 0.79 |
| Difference |  | 2.30 |
| Standard Error |  | 1.03 |
| 95% CI of difference |  | 0.24 to 4.35 |
| Test statistic t |  | 2.214 |
| Degrees of Freedom (DF) |  | 158 |
| Two-tailed probability |  | P<0.028 |

***Significant at 0.05 level**                    **Degree of freedom= 158**

Table-3 presents the results of Punjab boxers and Haryana boxers with regard to the variable Balance. The descriptive statistics shows the Mean and SD values of Punjab boxers on the sub-variable Balance as 26.70 and 6.03 respectively. However, Haryana boxers had Mean and SD values as 29.00 and 7.06 respectively. The Mean Difference and Standard Error Difference of Mean were 2.30 and 1.03 respectively. The 't'-value 2.214 as shown in the table above was found statistically significant (P<.05). But while comparing the mean values of both the groups, it has been observed that Haryana boxers have demonstrated better Balance than the Punjab boxers. The comparison of mean scores of both the groups has been presented graphically in figure-3.

**Table 4: Mean Values (±SD), Standard Error of the Mean and Test Statistic t of Coordination in Punjab Boxers (N = 80) and Haryana Boxers (N = 80).**

|  | Punjab Boxers | Haryana Boxers |
|---|---|---|
| Sample size | 80 | 80 |
| Arithmetic mean | 29.70 | 29.12 |
| 95% CI for the mean | 28.48 to 30.91 | 27.77 to 30.47 |
| Variance | 29.75 | 36.79 |
| Standard deviation | 5.45 | 6.06 |
| Standard error of the mean | 0.60 | 0.67 |
| Difference |  | 0.57 |
| Standard Error |  | 0.91 |
| 95% CI of difference |  | 2.37 to 1.22 |
| Test statistic t |  | 0.630 |
| Degrees of Freedom (DF) |  | 158 |
| Two-tailed probability |  | P>0.529 |

**\*Significant at 0.05 level**                    **Degree of freedom= 158**

Table-4 presents the results of Punjab boxers and Haryana boxers with regard to the variable Coordination. The descriptive statistics shows the Mean and SD values of Punjab boxers on the sub-variable Coordination as 29.70 and 5.45 respectively. However, Haryana boxers had Mean and SD values as 29.12 and 6.06 respectively. The Mean Difference and Standard Error Difference of Mean were 0.57 and 0.91 respectively. The 't'-value 0.630 as shown in the table above was found statistically insignificant (P>.05). But while comparing the mean values of both the groups, it has been observed that Haryana boxers have demonstrated better Coordination than the Punjab boxers. The comparison of mean scores of both the groups has been presented graphically in figure-4.

**Table 5: Mean Values (±SD), Standard Error of the Mean and Test Statistic t of Reaction Time in Punjab Boxers (N = 80) and Haryana Boxers (N = 80).**

|  | Punjab Boxers | Haryana Boxers |
|---|---|---|
| Sample size | 80 | 80 |
| Arithmetic mean | 0.22 | 0.23 |
| 95% CI for the mean | 0.22 to 0.23 | 0.22 to 0.23 |
| Variance | 0.0001 | 0.0001 |
| Standard deviation | 0.011 | 0.012 |
| Standard error of the mean | 0.0012 | 0.001 |
| Difference |  | 0.002 |
| Standard Error |  | 0.0018 |
| 95% CI of difference |  | 0.001to 0.005 |
| Test statistic t |  | 1.227 |
| Degrees of Freedom (DF) |  | 158 |
| Two-tailed probability |  | P>0.221 |

**\*Significant at 0.05 level**                              **Degree of freedom= 158**

Table-5 presents the results of Punjab boxers and Haryana boxers with regard to the variable Reaction Time. The descriptive statistics shows the Mean and SD values of Punjab boxers on the sub-variable Reaction Time as 0.22 and 0.01 respectively. However, Haryana boxers had Mean and SD values as 0.23 and 0.01 respectively. The Mean Difference and Standard Error Difference of Mean were 0.002 and 0.001 respectively. The't'-value 1.227 as shown in the table above was found statistically insignificant (P>.05). But while comparing the mean values of both the groups, it has been observed that Punjab boxers have demonstrated better Reaction Time than the Haryana boxers. The comparison of mean scores of both the groups has been presented graphically in figure-5.

**Table 6: Mean Values (±SD), Standard Error of the Mean and Test Statistic t of Power in Punjab Boxers (N = 80) and Haryana Boxers (N = 80).**

|  | Punjab Boxers | Haryana Boxers |
|---|---|---|
| Sample size | 80 | 80 |
| Arithmetic mean | 1.45 | 1.31 |
| 95% CI for the mean | 1.40 to 1.50 | 1.28 to 1.34 |
| Variance | 0.043 | 0.017 |
| Standard deviation | 0.20 | 0.13 |
| Standard error of the mean | 0.023 | 0.014 |
| Difference |  | 0.14 |
| Standard Error |  | 0.027 |
| 95% CI of difference |  | 0.19 to 0.085 |
| Test statistic t |  | 5.073 |
| Degrees of Freedom (DF) |  | 158 |
| Two-tailed probability |  | P < 0.000 |

**\*Significant at 0.05 level                    Degree of freedom= 158**

Table-6 presents the results of Punjab boxers and Haryana boxers with regard to the variable Power. The descriptive statistics shows the Mean and SD values of Punjab boxers on the sub-variable Power as 1.45 and 0.20 respectively. However, Haryana boxers had Mean and SD values as 1.31 and 0.13 respectively. The Mean Difference and Standard Error Difference of Mean were 0.14 and 0.027 respectively. The 't'-value 5.073 as shown in the table above was found statistically significant (P<.05). But while comparing the mean values of both the groups, it has been observed that Punjab boxers have demonstrated better Power than the Haryana boxers. The comparison of mean scores of both the groups has been presented graphically in figure-6.

**Table 7: Mean Values (±SD), Standard Error of the Mean and Test Statistic t of Vital Capacity in Punjab Boxers (N = 80) and Haryana Boxers (N = 80).**

|  | Punjab Boxers | Haryana Boxers |
|---|---|---|
| Sample size | 80 | 80 |
| Arithmetic mean | 3.57 | 3.69 |
| 95% CI for the mean | 3.50 to 3.65 | 3.61 to 3.76 |
| Variance | 0.11 | 0.10 |
| Standard deviation | 0.34 | 0.32 |
| Standard error of the mean | 0.038 | 0.036 |
| Difference |  | 0.11 |
| Standard Error |  | 0.053 |
| 95% CI of difference |  | 0.007 to 0.21 |
| Test statistic t |  | 2.116 |
| Degrees of Freedom (DF) |  | 158 |
| Two-tailed probability |  | P<0.03 |

**\*Significant at 0.05 level**                    **Degree of freedom= 158**

Table-7 presents the results of Punjab boxers and Haryana boxers with regard to the variable Vital Capacity. The descriptive statistics shows the Mean and SD values of Punjab boxers on the sub-variable Vital Capacity as 3.57 and 0.34 respectively. However, Haryana boxers had Mean and SD values as 3.69 and 0.32 respectively. The Mean Difference and Standard Error Difference of Mean were 0.11 and 0.053 respectively. The 't'-value 2.116 as shown in the table above was found statistically significant (P<.05). But while comparing the mean values of both the groups, it has been observed that Haryana boxers have demonstrated better Vital Capacity than the Punjab boxers. The comparison of mean scores of both the groups has been presented graphically in figure-7.

**Table 8: Mean Values (±SD), Standard Error of the Mean and Test Statistic t of Resting Pulse Rate in Punjab Boxers (N = 80) and Haryana Boxers (N = 80).**

|  | Punjab Boxers | Haryana Boxers |
|---|---|---|
| Sample size | 80 | 80 |
| Arithmetic mean | 76.91 | 74.32 |
| 95% CI for the mean | 76.20 to 77.61 | 73.69 to 74.95 |
| Variance | 10.00 | 8.09 |
| Standard deviation | 3.16 | 2.84 |
| Standard error of the mean | 0.35 | 0.31 |
| Difference |  | 2.58 |
| Standard Error |  | 0.47 |
| 95% CI of difference |  | 3.52 to 1.64 |
| Test statistic t |  | 5.440 |
| Degrees of Freedom (DF) |  | 158 |
| Two-tailed probability |  | P < 0.000 |

**\*Significant at 0.05 level**                    **Degree of freedom= 158**

Table-8 presents the results of Punjab boxers and Haryana boxers with regard to the variable Resting Pulse Rate. The descriptive statistics shows the Mean and SD values of Punjab boxers on the sub-variable Resting Pulse Rate as 76.91 and 3.16 respectively. However, Haryana boxers had Mean and SD values as 74.32 and 2.84 respectively. The Mean Difference and Standard Error Difference of Mean were 2.58 and 0.47 respectively. The 't'-value 5.440 as shown in the table above was found statistically significant (P<.05). But while comparing the mean values of both the groups, it has been observed that Haryana boxers have demonstrated better Resting Pulse Rate than the Punjab boxers. The comparison of mean scores of both the groups has been presented graphically in figure-8.

**Table 9: Mean Values (±SD), Standard Error of the Mean and Test Statistic t of Peak Flow Rate in Punjab Boxers (N = 80) and Haryana Boxers (N = 80).**

|  | Punjab Boxers | Haryana Boxers |
|---|---|---|
| Sample size | 80 | 80 |
| Arithmetic mean | 363.66 | 396.23 |
| 95% CI for the mean | 342.55 to 384.76 | 379.35 to 413.11 |
| Variance | 8995.77 | 5754.99 |
| Standard deviation | 94.84 | 75.86 |
| Standard error of the mean | 10.60 | 8.48 |
| Difference |  | 32.57 |
| Standard Error |  | 13.57 |
| 95% CI of difference |  | 5.75 to 59.39 |
| Test statistic t |  | 2.39 |
| Degrees of Freedom (DF) |  | 158 |
| Two-tailed probability |  | P<0.01 |

**\*Significant at 0.05 level**                  **Degree of freedom= 158**

Table-9 presents the results of Punjab boxers and Haryana boxers with regard to the variable Peak Flow Rate. The descriptive statistics shows the Mean and SD values of Punjab boxers on the sub-variable Peak Flow Rate as 363.66 and 94.84 respectively. However, Haryana boxers had Mean and SD values as 396.23 and 75.86 respectively. The Mean Difference and Standard Error Difference of Mean were 32.57 and 13.57 respectively. The 't'-value 2.399 as shown in the table above was found statistically significant (P<.05). But while comparing the mean values of both the groups, it has been observed that Haryana boxers have demonstrated better Peak Flow Rate than the Punjab boxers. The comparison of mean scores of both the groups has been presented graphically in figure-9.

**Table 10: Mean Values (±SD), Standard Error of the Mean and Test Statistic t of Standing Height in Punjab Boxers (N = 80) and Haryana Boxers (N = 80).**

|  | Punjab Boxers | Haryana Boxers |
|---|---|---|
| Sample size | 80 | 80 |
| Arithmetic mean | 174.65 | 172.67 |
| 95% CI for the mean | 173.58 to 175.71 | 171.41 to 173.93 |
| Variance | 22.7114 | 32.14 |
| Standard deviation | 4.76 | 5.66 |
| Standard error of the mean | 0.53 | 0.63 |
| Difference |  | 1.97 |
| Standard Error |  | 0.82 |
| 95% CI of difference |  | 3.61 to 0.33 |
| Test statistic t |  | 2.38 |
| Degrees of Freedom (DF) |  | 158 |
| Two-tailed probability |  | P<0.01 |

**\*Significant at 0.05 level**                    **Degree of freedom= 158**

Table-10 presents the results of Punjab boxers and Haryana boxers with regard to the variable Standing Height. The descriptive statistics shows the Mean and SD values of Punjab boxers on the sub-variable Standing Height as 174.65 and 4.76 respectively. However, Haryana boxers had Mean and SD values as 172.67 and 5.66 respectively. The Mean Difference and Standard Error Difference of Mean were 1.97 and 0.82 respectively. The't'-value 2.385 as shown in the table above was found statistically significant (P<.05). But while comparing the mean values of both the groups, it has been observed that Punjab boxers have demonstrated better Standing Height than the Haryana boxers. The comparison of mean scores of both the groups has been presented graphically in figure-10.

**Table 11: Mean Values (±SD), Standard Error of the Mean and Test Statistic t of Body Weight in Punjab Boxers (N = 80) and Haryana Boxers (N = 80).**

|  | Punjab Boxers | Haryana Boxers |
|---|---|---|
| Sample size | 80 | 80 |
| Arithmetic mean | 71.65 | 70.15 |
| 95% CI for the mean | 70.95 to 72.34 | 69.00 to 71.29 |
| Variance | 9.64 | 26.55 |
| Standard deviation | 3.10 | 5.15 |
| Standard error of the mean | 0.34 | 0.57 |
| Difference |  | 1.50 |
| Standard Error |  | 0.67 |
| 95% CI of difference |  | 2.82 to 0.17 |
| Test statistic t |  | 2.23 |
| Degrees of Freedom (DF) |  | 158 |
| Two-tailed probability |  | P<0.02 |

**\*Significant at 0.05 level**                    **Degree of freedom= 158**

Table-11 presents the results of Punjab boxers and Haryana boxers with regard to the variable Body Weight. The descriptive statistics shows the Mean and SD values of Punjab boxers on the sub-variable Body Weight as 71.65 and 3.10 respectively. However, Haryana boxers had Mean and SD values as 70.15 and 5.15 respectively. The Mean Difference and Standard Error Difference of Mean were 1.50 and 0.67 respectively. The 't'-value 2.230 as shown in the table above was found statistically significant ($P<.05$). But while comparing the mean values of both the groups, it has been observed that Haryana boxers have demonstrated better Body Weight than the Punjab boxers. The comparison of mean scores of both the groups has been presented graphically in figure-11.

**Table 12: Mean Values (±SD), Standard Error of the Mean and Test Statistic t of Leg Length in Punjab Boxers (N = 80) and Haryana Boxers (N = 80).**

|  | Punjab Boxers | Haryana Boxers |
|---|---|---|
| Sample size | 80 | 80 |
| Arithmetic mean | 101.30 | 100.30 |
| 95% CI for the mean | 100.41 to 102.19 | 99.17 to 101.42 |
| Variance | 15.87 | 25.74 |
| Standard deviation | 3.98 | 5.07 |
| Standard error of the mean | 0.44 | 0.56 |
| Difference |  | 1.00 |
| Standard Error |  | 0.72 |
| 95% CI of difference |  | 2.43 to 0.41 |
| Test statistic t |  | 1.39 |
| Degrees of Freedom (DF) |  | 158 |
| Two-tailed probability |  | P>0.16 |

**\*Significant at 0.05 level**          **Degree of freedom= 158**

Table-12 presents the results of Punjab boxers and Haryana boxers with regard to the variable Leg Length. The descriptive statistics shows the Mean and SD values of Punjab boxers on the sub-variable Leg Length as 101.30 and 3.98 respectively. However, Haryana boxers had Mean and SD values as 100.30 and 5.07 respectively. The Mean Difference and Standard Error Difference of Mean were 1.00 and 0.72 respectively. The 't'-value 1.395 as shown in the table above was found statistically insignificant (P>.05). But while comparing the mean values of both the groups, it has been observed that Punjab boxers have demonstrated better Leg Length than the Haryana boxers. The comparison of mean scores of both the groups has been presented graphically in figure-12.

**Table 13: Mean Values (±SD), Standard Error of the Mean and Test Statistic t of Upper Leg Length in Punjab Boxers (N = 80) and Haryana Boxers (N = 80).**

|  | Punjab Boxers | Haryana Boxers |
|---|---|---|
| Sample size | 80 | 80 |
| Arithmetic mean | 50.76 | 50.15 |
| 95% CI for the mean | 50.27 to 51.26 | 49.65 to 50.64 |
| Variance | 4.93 | 4.86 |
| Standard deviation | 2.22 | 2.20 |
| Standard error of the mean | 0.24 | 0.24 |
| Difference | | 0.61 |
| Standard Error | | 0.35 |
| 95% CI of difference | | 1.31 to 0.072 |
| Test statistic t | | 1.768 |
| Degrees of Freedom (DF) | | 158 |
| Two-tailed probability | | P>0.07 |

**\*Significant at 0.05 level**         **Degree of freedom= 158**

Table-13 presents the results of Punjab boxers and Haryana boxers with regard to the variable Upper Leg Length. The descriptive statistics shows the Mean and SD values of Punjab boxers on the sub-variable Upper Leg Length as 50.76 and 2.22 respectively. However, Haryana boxers had Mean and SD values as 50.15 and 2.20 respectively. The Mean Difference and Standard Error Difference of Mean were 0.61 and 0.35 respectively. The 't'-value 1.768 as shown in the table above was found statistically insignificant (P>.05). But while comparing the mean values of both the groups, it has been observed that Punjab boxers have demonstrated better Upper Leg Length than the Haryana boxers. The comparison of mean scores of both the groups has been presented graphically in figure-13.

**Table 14: Mean Values (±SD), Standard Error of the Mean and Test Statistic t of Lower Leg Length in Punjab Boxers (N = 80) and Haryana Boxers (N = 80).**

| | Punjab Boxers | Haryana Boxers |
|---|---|---|
| Sample size | 80 | 80 |
| Arithmetic mean | 50.55 | 49.15 |
| 95% CI for the mean | 50.11 to 50.99 | 48.56 to 49.73 |
| Variance | 3.94 | 6.80 |
| Standard deviation | 1.98 | 2.60 |
| Standard error of the mean | 0.22 | 0.29 |
| Difference | | 1.40 |
| Standard Error | | 0.36 |
| 95% CI of difference | | 2.13 to 0.68 |
| Test statistic t | | 3.837 |
| Degrees of Freedom (DF) | | 158 |
| Two-tailed probability | | P<0.00 |

**\*Significant at 0.05 level**                    **Degree of freedom= 158**

Table-14 presents the results of Punjab boxers and Haryana boxers with regard to the variable Lower Leg Length. The descriptive statistics shows the Mean and SD values of Punjab boxers on the sub-variable Lower Leg Length as 50.55 and 1.98 respectively. However, Haryana boxers had Mean and SD values as 49.15 and 2.60 respectively. The Mean Difference and Standard Error Difference of Mean were 1.40 and 0.36 respectively. The 't'-value 3.837 as shown in the table above was found statistically significant (P<.05). But while comparing the mean values of both the groups, it has been observed that Punjab boxers have demonstrated better Lower Leg Length than the Haryana boxers. The comparison of mean scores of both the groups has been presented graphically in figure-14.

**Table 15: Mean Values (±SD), Standard Error of the Mean and Test Statistic t of Arm Length in Punjab Boxers (N = 80) and Haryana Boxers (N = 80).**

|  | Punjab Boxers | Haryana Boxers |
|---|---|---|
| Sample size | 80 | 80 |
| Arithmetic mean | 82.15 | 80.76 |
| 95% CI for the mean | 81.63 to 82.66 | 80.04 to 81.47 |
| Variance | 5.45 | 10.29 |
| Standard deviation | 2.33 | 3.20 |
| Standard error of the mean | 0.26 | 0.35 |
| Difference |  | 1.38 |
| Standard Error |  | 0.44 |
| 95% CI of difference |  | 2.26 to 0.51 |
| Test statistic t |  | 3.127 |
| Degrees of Freedom (DF) |  | 158 |
| Two-tailed probability |  | P<0.00 |

**\*Significant at 0.05 level                    Degree of freedom= 158**

Table-15 presents the results of Punjab boxers and Haryana boxers with regard to the variable Arm Length. The descriptive statistics shows the Mean and SD values of Punjab boxers on the sub-variable Arm Length as 82.15 and 2.33 respectively. However, Haryana boxers had Mean and SD values as 80.76 and 3.20 respectively. The Mean Difference and Standard Error Difference of Mean were 1.38 and 0.44 respectively. The 't'-value 3.127 as shown in the table above was found statistically significant (P<.05). But while comparing the mean values of both the groups, it has been observed that Punjab boxers have demonstrated better Arm Length than the Haryana boxers. The comparison of mean scores of both the groups has been presented graphically in figure-15.

**Table 16: Mean Values (±SD), Standard Error of the Mean and Test Statistic t of Upper Arm Length in Punjab Boxers (N = 80) and Haryana Boxers (N = 80).**

|  | Punjab Boxers | Haryana Boxers |
|---|---|---|
| Sample size | 80 | 80 |
| Arithmetic mean | 36.14 | 35.66 |
| 95% CI for the mean | 35.86 to 36.42 | 35.29 to 36.03 |
| Variance | 1.60 | 2.78 |
| Standard deviation | 1.26 | 1.66 |
| Standard error of the mean | 0.14 | 0.18 |
| Difference | | 0.48 |
| Standard Error | | 0.23 |
| 95% CI of difference | | 0.940 to 0.018 |
| Test statistic t | | 2.054 |
| Degrees of Freedom (DF) | | 158 |
| Two-tailed probability | | P<0.0416 |

**\*Significant at 0.05 level**                         **Degree of freedom= 158**

Table-16 presents the results of Punjab boxers and Haryana boxers with regard to the variable Upper Arm Length. The descriptive statistics shows the Mean and SD values of Punjab boxers on the sub-variable Upper Arm Length as 36.14 and 1.26 respectively. However, Haryana boxers had Mean and SD values as 35.66 and 1.66 respectively. The Mean Difference and Standard Error Difference of Mean were 0.48 and 0.23 respectively. The 't'-value 2.054 as shown in the table above was found statistically significant (P<.05). But while comparing the mean values of both the groups, it has been observed that Punjab boxers have demonstrated better Upper Arm Length than the Haryana boxers. The comparison of mean scores of both the groups has been presented graphically in figure-16.

**Table 17: Mean Values (±SD), Standard Error of the Mean and Test Statistic t of Lower Arm Length in Punjab Boxers (N = 80) and Haryana Boxers (N = 80).**

|  | Punjab Boxers | Haryana Boxers |
|---|---|---|
| Sample size | 80 | 80 |
| Arithmetic mean | 46.59 | 44.92 |
| 95% CI for the mean | 45.94 to 47.24 | 44.54 to 45.30 |
| Variance | 8.62 | 2.89 |
| Standard deviation | 2.93 | 1.70 |
| Standard error of the mean | 0.32 | 0.19 |
| Difference |  | 1.66 |
| Standard Error |  | 0.37 |
| 95% CI of difference |  | 2.41 to 0.91 |
| Test statistic t |  | 4.398 |
| Degrees of Freedom (DF) |  | 158 |
| Two-tailed probability |  | P<0.000 |

**\*Significant at 0.05 level**                    **Degree of freedom= 158**

Table-17 presents the results of Punjab boxers and Haryana boxers with regard to the variable Lower Arm Length. The descriptive statistics shows the Mean and SD values of Punjab boxers on the sub-variable Lower Arm Length as 46.59 and 2.93 respectively. However, Haryana boxers had Mean and SD values as 44.92 and 1.70 respectively. The Mean Difference and Standard Error Difference of Mean were 1.66 and 0.37 respectively. The 't'-value 4.398 as shown in the table above was found statistically significant (P<.05). But while comparing the mean values of both the groups, it has been observed that Punjab boxers have demonstrated better Lower Arm Length than the Haryana boxers. The comparison of mean scores of both the groups has been presented graphically in figure-17.

**Table 18: Mean Values (±SD), Standard Error of the Mean and Test Statistic t Hip width in Punjab Boxers (N = 80) and Haryana Boxers (N = 80).**

|  | Punjab Boxers | Haryana Boxers |
|---|---|---|
| Sample size | 80 | 80 |
| Arithmetic mean | 30.95 | 31.00 |
| 95% CI for the mean | 30.38 to 31.51 | 30.51 to 31.48 |
| Variance | 6.55 | 4.69 |
| Standard deviation | 2.56 | 2.16 |
| Standard error of the mean | 0.28 | 0.24 |
| Difference |  | 0.050 |
| Standard Error |  | 0.37 |
| 95% CI of difference |  | 0.69 to 0.79 |
| Test statistic t |  | 0.133 |
| Degrees of Freedom (DF) |  | 158 |
| Two-tailed probability |  | P>0.8941 |

**\*Significant at 0.05 level**                                **Degree of freedom= 158**

Table-18 presents the results of Punjab boxers and Haryana boxers with regard to the variable Hip Width. The descriptive statistics shows the Mean and SD values of Punjab boxers on the sub-variable Hip Width as 30.95 and 2.56 respectively. However, Haryana boxers had Mean and SD values as 31.00 and 2.16 respectively. The Mean Difference and Standard Error Difference of Mean were 0.050 and 0.37 respectively. The 't'-value 0.133 as shown in the table above was found statistically insignificant (P>.05). But while comparing the mean values of both the groups, it has been observed that Haryana boxers have demonstrated better Hip Width than the Punjab boxers. The comparison of mean scores of both the groups has been presented graphically in figure 18.

**Table 19: Mean Values (±SD), Standard Error of the Mean and Test Statistic t Shoulder width in Punjab Boxers (N = 80) and Haryana Boxers (N = 80).**

| | Punjab Boxers | Haryana Boxers |
|---|---|---|
| Sample size | 80 | 80 |
| Arithmetic mean | 35.45 | 34.96 |
| 95% CI for the mean | 35.02 to 35.87 | 34.66 to 35.26 |
| Variance | 3.57 | 1.79 |
| Standard deviation | 1.89 | 1.34 |
| Standard error of the mean | 0.21 | 0.14 |
| Difference | | 0.48 |
| Standard Error | | 0.25 |
| 95% CI of difference | | 0.99 to 0.024 |
| Test statistic t | | 1.881 |
| Degrees of Freedom (DF) | | 158 |
| Two-tailed probability | | P>0.0619 |

**\*Significant at 0.05 level**            **Degree of freedom= 158**

Table-19 presents the results of Punjab boxers and Haryana boxers with regard to the variable Shoulder Width. The descriptive statistics shows the Mean and SD values of Punjab boxers on the sub-variable Shoulder Width as 35.45 and 1.89 respectively. However, Haryana boxers had Mean and SD values as 34.96 and 1.34 respectively. The Mean Difference and Standard Error Difference of Mean were 0.48 and 0.25 respectively. The't'-value 1.881 as shown in the table above was found statistically insignificant (P>.05). But while comparing the mean values of both the groups, it has been observed that Punjab boxers have demonstrated better Shoulder Width than the Haryana boxers. The comparison of mean scores of both the groups has been presented graphically in figure-19.

**Table 20: Mean Values (±SD), Standard Error of the Mean and Test Statistic t Chest Width in Punjab Boxers (N = 80) and Haryana Boxers (N = 80).**

|  | Punjab Boxers | Haryana Boxers |
|---|---|---|
| Sample size | 80 | 80 |
| Arithmetic mean | 31.05 | 30.22 |
| 95% CI for the mean | 30.62 to 31.47 | 29.77 to 30.67 |
| Variance | 3.63 | 4.12 |
| Standard deviation | 1.90 | 2.03 |
| Standard error of the mean | 0.21 | 0.22 |
| Difference |  | 0.82 |
| Standard Error |  | 0.31 |
| 95% CI of difference |  | 1.44 to 0.21 |
| Test statistic t |  | 2.650 |
| Degrees of Freedom (DF) |  | 158 |
| Two-tailed probability |  | P>0.0089 |

**\*Significant at 0.05 level          Degree of freedom= 158**

Table-20 presents the results of Punjab boxers and Haryana boxers with regard to the variable Chest Width. The descriptive statistics shows the Mean and SD values of Punjab boxers on the sub-variable Chest Width as 31.05 and 1.90 respectively. However, Haryana boxers had Mean and SD values as 30.22 and 2.03 respectively. The Mean Difference and Standard Error Difference of Mean were 0.82 and 0.31 respectively. The 't'-value 2.650 as shown in the table above was found statistically insignificant (P>.05). But while comparing the mean values of both the groups, it has been observed that Punjab boxers have demonstrated better Chest Width than the Haryana boxers. The comparison of mean scores of both the groups has been presented graphically in figure-20.

**Table 21: Mean Values (±SD), Standard Error of the Mean and Test Statistic t Calf Girth in Punjab Boxers (N = 80) and Haryana Boxers (N = 80).**

|  | Punjab Boxers | Haryana Boxers |
|---|---|---|
| Sample size | 80 | 80 |
| Arithmetic mean | 38.71 | 32.54 |
| 95% CI for the mean | 38.32 to 39.10 | 32.12 to 32.95 |
| Variance | 3.10 | 3.48 |
| Standard deviation | 1.76 | 1.86 |
| Standard error of the mean | 0.19 | 0.20 |
| Difference |  | 6.17 |
| Standard Error |  | 0.28 |
| 95% CI of difference |  | 6.73 to 5.60 |
| Test statistic t |  | 21.49 |
| Degrees of Freedom (DF) |  | 158 |
| Two-tailed probability |  | P < 0.0001 |

**\*Significant at 0.05 level**                    **Degree of freedom= 158**

Table-21 presents the results of Punjab boxers and Haryana boxers with regard to the variable Calf Girth. The descriptive statistics shows the Mean and SD values of Punjab boxers on the sub-variable Calf Girth as 38.71 and 1.76 respectively. However, Haryana boxers had Mean and SD values as 32.54 and 1.86 respectively. The Mean Difference and Standard Error Difference of Mean were 6.17 and 0.28 respectively. The 't'-value 21.49 as shown in the table above was found statistically significant (P<.05). But while comparing the mean values of both the groups, it has been observed that Punjab boxers have demonstrated better Calf Girth than the Haryana boxers. The comparison of mean scores of both the groups has been presented graphically in figure-21.

**Table 22: Mean Values (±SD), Standard Error of the Mean and Test Statistic t Thigh Girth in Punjab Boxers (N = 80) and Haryana Boxers (N = 80).**

|  | Punjab Boxers | Haryana Boxers |
|---|---|---|
| Sample size | 80 | 80 |
| Arithmetic mean | 55.58 | 51.51 |
| 95% CI for the mean | 55.14 to 56.02 | 50.90 to 52.12 |
| Variance | 3.97 | 7.46 |
| Standard deviation | 1.99 | 2.73 |
| Standard error of the mean | 0.22 | 0.30 |
| Difference |  | 4.07 |
| Standard Error |  | 0.37 |
| 95% CI of difference |  | 4.81 to 3.32 |
| Test statistic t |  | 10.71 |
| Degrees of Freedom (DF) |  | 158 |
| Two-tailed probability |  | P<0.00 |

**\*Significant at 0.05 level**          **Degree of freedom= 158**

Table-22 presents the results of Punjab boxers and Haryana boxers with regard to the variable Thigh Girth. The descriptive statistics shows the Mean and SD values of Punjab boxers on the sub-variable Thigh Girth as 55.58 and 1.99 respectively. However, Haryana boxers had Mean and SD values as 51.51 and 2.73 respectively. The Mean Difference and Standard Error Difference of Mean were 4.07 and 0.37 respectively. The 't'-value 10.771 as shown in the table above was found statistically significant (P<.05). But while comparing the mean values of both the groups, it has been observed that Punjab boxers have demonstrated better Thigh Girth than the Haryana boxers. The comparison of mean scores of both the groups has been presented graphically in figure-22.

**Table 23: Mean Values (±SD), Standard Error of the Mean and Test Statistic t Chest Girth in Punjab Boxers (N = 80) and Haryana Boxers (N = 80).**

|  | Punjab Boxers | Haryana Boxers |
|---|---|---|
| Sample size | 80 | 80 |
| Arithmetic mean | 90.40 | 88.95 |
| 95% CI for the mean | 89.72 to 91.07 | 88.02 to 89.87 |
| Variance | 9.26 | 17.36 |
| Standard deviation | 3.04 | 4.16 |
| Standard error of the mean | 0.34 | 0.46 |
| Difference |  | 1.45 |
| Standard Error |  | 0.57 |
| 95% CI of difference |  | 2.5896 to 0.31 |
| Test statistic t |  | 2.513 |
| Degrees of Freedom (DF) |  | 158 |
| Two-tailed probability |  | P<0.01 |

**\*Significant at 0.05 level**                                              **Degree of freedom= 158**

Table-23 presents the results of Punjab boxers and Haryana boxers with regard to the variable Chest Girth. The descriptive statistics shows the Mean and SD values of Punjab boxers on the sub-variable Chest Girth as 90.40 and 3.04 respectively. However, Haryana boxers had Mean and SD values as 88.95 and 4.16 respectively. The Mean Difference and Standard Error Difference of Mean were 1.45 and 0.57 respectively. The 't'-value 2.513 as shown in the table above was found statistically significant (P<.05). But while comparing the mean values of both the groups, it has been observed that Punjab boxers have demonstrated better Chest Girth than the Haryana boxers. The comparison of mean scores of both the groups has been presented graphically in figure-23.

**Table 24: Mean Values (±SD), Standard Error of the Mean and Test Statistic t Upper Arm Girth in Punjab Boxers (N = 80) and Haryana Boxers (N = 80).**

|  | Punjab Boxers | Haryana Boxers |
|---|---|---|
| Sample size | 80 | 80 |
| Arithmetic mean | 29.32 | 25.92 |
| 95% CI for the mean | 28.84 to 29.79 | 25.67 to 26.17 |
| Variance | 4.56 | 1.29 |
| Standard deviation | 2.13 | 1.13 |
| Standard error of the mean | 0.23 | 0.12 |
| Difference |  | 3.39 |
| Standard Error |  | 0.27 |
| 95% CI of difference |  | 3.93 to 2.86 |
| Test statistic t |  | 12.550 |
| Degrees of Freedom (DF) |  | 158 |
| Two-tailed probability |  | P < 0.00 |

**\*Significant at 0.05 level**                                          **Degree of freedom= 158**

Table-24 presents the results of Punjab boxers and Haryana boxers with regard to the variable Upper Arm Girth. The descriptive statistics shows the Mean and SD values of Punjab boxers on the sub-variable Upper Arm Girth as 29.32 and 2.13 respectively. However, Haryana boxers had Mean and SD values as 25.92 and 1.13 respectively. The Mean Difference and Standard Error Difference of Mean were 3.39 and 0.27 respectively. The 't'-value 12.550 as shown in the table above was found statistically significant (P<.05). But while comparing the mean values of both the groups, it has been observed that Punjab boxers have demonstrated better Upper Arm Girth than the Haryana boxers. The comparison of mean scores of both the groups has been presented graphically in figure-24.

**Table 25: Mean Values (±SD), Standard Error of the Mean and Test Statistic t Lower Arm Girth in Punjab Boxers (N = 80) and Haryana Boxers (N = 80).**

|  | Punjab Boxers | Haryana Boxers |
|---|---|---|
| Sample size | 80 | 80 |
| Arithmetic mean | 25.86 | 25.04 |
| 95% CI for the mean | 25.59 to 26.12 | 24.77 to 25.31 |
| Variance | 1.44 | 1.44 |
| Standard deviation | 1.20 | 1.20 |
| Standard error of the mean | 0.13 | 0.13 |
| Difference |  | 0.81 |
| Standard Error |  | 0.19 |
| 95% CI of difference |  | 1.19 to 0.43 |
| Test statistic t |  | 4.286 |
| Degrees of Freedom (DF) |  | 158 |
| Two-tailed probability |  | P<0.0001 |

**\*Significant at 0.05 level**                    **Degree of freedom= 158**

Table-25 presents the results of Punjab boxers and Haryana boxers with regard to the variable Lower Arm Girth. The descriptive statistics shows the Mean and SD values of Punjab boxers on the sub-variable Lower Arm Girth as 25.86 and 1.20 respectively. However, Haryana boxers had Mean and SD values as 25.04 and 120 respectively. The Mean Difference and Standard Error Difference of Mean were 0.81 and 0.19 respectively. The't'-value 4.286 as shown in the table above was found statistically significant (P<.05). But while comparing the mean values of both the groups, it has been observed that Punjab boxers have demonstrated better Lower Arm Girth than the Haryana boxers. The comparison of mean scores of both the groups has been presented graphically in figure-25.

**Table 26: Mean Values (±SD), Standard Error of the Mean and Test Statistic t of Physical Fitness Components (i.e., Speed, Agility, Balance, Coordination, Reaction Time and Power) in Punjab Boxers (N = 80) and Haryana Boxers (N = 80).**

| Variables | Punjab Boxers ($N_1$=80) | | Haryana Boxers ($N_2$=80) | | | | | |
|-----------|------|------|------|------|-----------------|------|---------|------|
|           | Mean | SD   | Mean | SD   | Mean Difference | SEDM | t-value | Sig. |
| Speed     | 8.02 | 0.53 | 7.87 | 0.27 | 0.15  | 0.06  | 2.28* | 0.02 |
| Agility   | 14.08| 0.37 | 14.00| 0.18 | 0.079 | 0.04  | 1.71  | 0.08 |
| Balance   | 26.70| 6.03 | 29.00| 7.06 | 2.30  | 1.03  | 2.21* | 0.02 |
| Coordination | 29.70 | 5.45 | 29.12 | 6.06 | 0.57 | 0.91 | 0.63 | 0.52 |
| Reaction Time | 0.22 | 0.01 | 0.23 | 0.01 | 0.002 | 0.001 | 1.22 | 0.22 |
| Power     | 1.45 | 0.20 | 1.31 | 0.13 | 0.14  | 0.02  | 5.07* | 0.00 |

**\*Significant at 0.05 level**                    **Degree of freedom= 158**

The results of physical fitness components between Punjab boxers and Haryana boxers are presented in table-26. Analysis of data revealed significant between-group differences were found for speed (P<.05), balance (P<.05) and power (P<.05). Thus it may be concluded that speed, balance and power between Punjab boxers and Haryana boxers found to be statistically significant whereas insignificant between-group differences were found for agility (P>.05), coordination (P>.05) and reaction time (P>.05). Thus it may be concluded that agility, coordination and reaction time between Punjab boxers and Haryana boxers found to be statistically insignificant. The comparison of mean and SD scores of both the groups has been presented graphically in figure-26.

**Table 27: Mean Values (±SD), Standard Error of the Mean and Test Statistic t of Physiological Characteristics (i.e., Vital Capacity, Pulse Rate and Peak Flow Rate) in Punjab Boxers (N = 80) and Haryana Boxers (N = 80).**

| Variables | Punjab Boxers ($N_1$=80) | | Haryana Boxers ($N_2$=80) | | | | | |
|---|---|---|---|---|---|---|---|---|
| | Mean | SD | Mean | SD | Mean Difference | SEDM | t-value | Sig. |
| Vital Capacity | 3.57 | 0.34 | 3.69 | 0.32 | 0.11 | 0.05 | 2.11* | 0.03 |
| Resting Pulse Rate | 76.9 | 3.16 | 74.32 | 2.84 | 2.58 | 0.47 | 5.44* | 0.00 |
| Peak Flow Rate | 363.66 | 94.84 | 396.23 | 75.86 | 32.57 | 13.57 | 2.39* | 0.01 |

**\*Significant at 0.05 level**          **Degree of freedom= 158**

The results of physiological characteristics between Punjab boxers and Haryana boxers are presented in table-27. Analysis of data revealed significant between-group differences were found for vital capacity (P<.05), resting pulse rate (P<.05) and peak flow rate (P<.05). Thus it may be concluded that vital capacity, resting pulse rate and peak flow rate between Punjab boxers and Haryana boxers found to be statistically significant. The comparison of mean and SD scores of both the groups has been presented graphically in figure-27.

**Table 28: Mean Values (±SD), Standard Error of the Mean and Test Statistic t of Anthropometric Characteristics (i.e., Standing Height, Weight, Leg Length, Upper Leg Length, Lower Leg Length, Arm Length, Upper Arm Length, Lower Arm Length, Hip Width, Shoulder Width, Chest Width, Calf Girth, Thigh Girth, Chest Girth, Upper Arm Girth and Lower Arm Girth) in Punjab Boxers (N = 80) and Haryana Boxers (N = 80).**

| Variables | Punjab Boxers ($N_1$=80) | | Haryana Boxers ($N_2$=80) | | | | | |
|---|---|---|---|---|---|---|---|---|
| | Mean | SD | Mean | SD | Mean Difference | SEDM | t-value | Sig. |
| Standing Height | 174.65 | 4.76 | 172.67 | 5.66 | 1.97 | 0.82 | 2.38 | 0.01 |
| Weight | 71.65 | 3.10 | 70.15 | 5.15 | 1.50 | 0.67 | 2.23 | 0.02 |
| Leg Length | 101.30 | 3.98 | 100.30 | 5.07 | 1.00 | 0.72 | 1.39 | 0.16 |

| | | | | | | | | |
|---|---|---|---|---|---|---|---|---|
| Upper Leg Length | 50.76 | 2.22 | 50.15 | 2.20 | 0.61 | 0.35 | 1.76 | 0.07 |
| Lower Leg Length | 50.55 | 1.98 | 49.15 | 2.60 | 1.40 | 0.36 | 3.83 | 0.00 |
| Arm Length | 82.15 | 2.33 | 80.76 | 3.20 | 1.38 | 0.44 | 3.12 | 0.00 |
| Upper Arm Length | 36.14 | 1.26 | 35.66 | 1.66 | 0.48 | 0.23 | 2.05 | 0.04 |
| Lower Arm Length | 46.59 | 2.93 | 44.92 | 1.70 | 1.66 | 0.37 | 4.39 | 0.00 |
| Hip width | 30.95 | 2.56 | 31.00 | 2.16 | 0.05 | 0.37 | 0.13 | 0.89 |
| Shoulder width | 35.45 | 1.89 | 34.96 | 1.34 | 0.48 | 0.25 | 1.88 | 0.06 |
| Chest Width | 31.05 | 1.90 | 30.22 | 2.03 | 0.82 | 0.31 | 2.65 | 0.00 |
| Calf Girth | 38.71 | 1.76 | 32.54 | 1.86 | 6.17 | 0.28 | 21.49 | 0.00 |
| Thigh Girth | 55.58 | 1.99 | 51.51 | 2.73 | 4.072 | 0.37 | 10.77 | 0.00 |
| Chest Girth | 90.40 | 3.04 | 88.95 | 4.16 | 1.45 | 0.57 | 2.51 | 0.01 |
| Upper Arm Girth | 29.32 | 2.13 | 25.92 | 1.13 | 3.39 | 0.27 | 12.55 | 0.00 |
| Lower Arm Girth | 25.86 | 1.20 | 25.04 | 1.20 | 0.81 | 0.19 | 4.28 | 0.00 |

**\*Significant at 0.05 level**                                    **Degree of freedom= 158**

The results of anthropometric characteristics between Punjab boxers and Haryana boxers are presented in table-28. Analysis of data revealed significant between-group differences were found for standing height ($P<.05$), weight ($P<.05$), lower leg length ($P<.05$), arm length ($P<.05$), upper arm length ($P<.05$), lower arm length ($P<.05$), chest width ($P<.05$), calf girth ($P<.05$), thigh girth ($P<.05$), chest girth ($P<.05$), upper arm girth ($P<.05$) and lower arm girth ($P<.05$). Thus it may be concluded that standing height, weight, lower leg length, arm length, upper arm length, lower arm length, chest width, calf girth, thigh girth, chest girth, upper arm girth and lower arm girth between Punjab boxers and Haryana boxers found to be statistically significant whereas insignificant between-group differences were found for Leg Length ($P>.05$), Upper Leg Length ($P>.05$), Hip width ($P>.05$) and Shoulder width ($P>.05$). Thus it may be concluded that Leg Length, Upper Leg Length, Hip width and Shoulder width between Punjab boxers and Haryana boxers found to be statistically insignificant. The comparison of mean and SD scores of both the groups has been presented graphically in figure-28.

# Chapter - V

## Summary, Findings, Conclusion and Recommendations

### SUMMARY

The purpose of the study was to find out the difference of Physical, Physiological and Anthropometric Characteristics of Punjab and Haryana Boxers with the objectives:

1. To find out the significant difference of Physical Fitness Components (i.e., Speed, Agility, Balance, Coordination, Reaction Time and Power) among Punjab and Haryana boxers.

2. To find out the significant difference of Physiological Characteristics (i.e., Vital Capacity, Pulse Rate and Peak Flow Rate) among Punjab and Haryana boxers.

3. To find out the significant differences of Anthropometric Characteristics (i.e., Standing Height, Weight, Leg Length, Upper Leg Length, Lower Leg Length, Arm Length, Upper Arm Length, Lower Arm Length, Hip Width, Shoulder Width, Chest Width, Calf Girth, Thigh Girth, Chest Girth, Upper Arm Girth and Lower Arm Girth) among Punjab and Haryana boxers.

It was hypothesized that:

1. There would be no significant difference of Physical Fitness Components (i.e., Speed, Agility, Balance, Coordination, Reaction Time and Power) among Punjab and Haryana boxers.

2. There would be no significant difference of Physiological Characteristics (i.e., Vital Capacity, Pulse Rate and Peak Flow Rate) among Punjab and Haryana boxers.

3.    There would be no significant differences of Anthropometric Characteristics (i.e., Standing Height, Weight, Leg Length, Upper Leg Length, Lower Leg Length, Arm Length, Upper Arm Length, Lower Arm Length, Hip Width, Shoulder Width,

Chest Width, Calf Girth, Thigh Girth, Chest Girth, Upper Arm Girth and Lower Arm Girth) among Punjab and Haryana boxers.

For the purpose of the present study, One Hundred Sixty (N=160) subjects between the age group of 19-28 years were selected. The subjects were purposively assigned into two groups: Group-A: Punjab Boxers ($N_1$=80) and Group-B: Haryana Boxers ($N_2$=80). All the subjects were informed about the objective and protocol of the study.

The following variables were selected for the present study:

I. Physical Fitness Components:
    i. Speed
    ii. Agility
    iii. Balance
    iv. Coordination
    v. Reaction Time
    vi. Power

II. Physiological Characteristics:
    i. Vital Capacity
    ii. Resting Pulse Rate
    iii. Peak Flow Rate

III. Anthropometric Characteristics:
    i. Standing height
    ii. Body weight
    iii. Leg length
    iv. Upper leg length
    v. Lower leg length
    vi. Arm length
    vii. Upper arm length
    viii. Lower arm length
    ix. Hip width (bitrochantric diameter)
    x. Shoulder width (biacromial diameter)
    xi. Chest width
    xii. Calf girth
    xiii. Thigh girth
    xiv. Chest girth

xv.    Upper arm girth

xvi.    Lower arm girth

The Statistical Package for the Social Sciences (SPSS) version 14.0 was used for all analyses. The differences in the mean of each group for selected variable were tested for the significance of difference by t-test. In all the analyses, the 5% critical level (p<0.05) was considered to indicate statistical significance.

# FINDINGS

## Findings with regard to the variable Physical Fitness Components between Punjab Boxers and Haryana Boxers

The results of physical fitness components between Punjab boxers and Haryana boxers are presented in table-26. Analysis of data revealed significant between-group differences were found for speed (P<.05), balance (P<.05) and power (P<.05). Thus it may be concluded that speed, balance and power between Punjab boxers and Haryana boxers found to be statistically significant whereas insignificant between-group differences were found for agility (P>.05), coordination (P>.05) and reaction time (P>.05). Thus it may be concluded that agility, coordination and reaction time between Punjab boxers and Haryana boxers found to be statistically insignificant.

## Findings with regard to the variable Physiological Characteristics between Punjab Boxers and Haryana Boxers

The results of physiological characteristics between Punjab boxers and Haryana boxers are presented in table-27. Analysis of data revealed significant between-group differences were found for vital capacity (P<.05), resting pulse rate (P<.05) and peak flow rate (P<.05). Thus it may be concluded that vital capacity, resting pulse rate and peak flow rate between Punjab boxers and Haryana boxers found to be statistically significant.

## Findings with regard to the variable Anthropometric Characteristics between Punjab boxers and Haryana boxers

The results of anthropometric characteristics between Punjab boxers and Haryana boxers are presented in table-28. Analysis of data revealed significant between-group differences were found for standing height (P<.05), weight (P<.05), lower leg length (P<.05), arm length (P<.05), upper arm length (P<.05), lower arm length (P<.05), chest width (P<.05), calf girth (P<.05), thigh girth (P<.05), chest girth

(P<.05), upper arm girth (P<.05) and lower arm girth (P<.05). Thus it may be concluded that standing height, weight, lower leg length, arm length, upper arm length, lower arm length, chest width, calf girth, thigh girth, chest girth, upper arm girth and lower arm girth between Punjab boxers and Haryana boxers found to be statistically significant whereas insignificant between-group differences were found for Leg Length (P>.05), Upper Leg Length (P>.05), Hip width (P>.05) and Shoulder width (P>.05). Thus it may be concluded that Leg Length, Upper Leg Length, Hip width and Shoulder width between Punjab boxers and Haryana boxers found to be statistically insignificant.

## CONCLUSIONS OF THE STUDY

*Based on the findings of this study, the following conclusions were drawn:*

1.  The Mean and SD values of Punjab boxers on the sub-variable Speed as 8.02 and 0.53 respectively. However, Haryana boxers had Mean and SD values as 7.87 and 0.27 respectively. The Mean Difference and Standard Error Difference of Mean were 0.15 and 0.06 respectively. The't'-value 2.289 as shown in the table above was found statistically significant (P<.05). But while comparing the mean values of both the groups, it has been observed that Haryana boxers have demonstrated better Speed than the Punjab boxers.

2.  The Mean and SD values of Punjab boxers on the sub-variable Agility as 14.08 and 0.37 respectively. However, Haryana boxers had Mean and SD values as 14.00 and 0.18 respectively. The Mean Difference and Standard Error Difference of Mean were 0.07 and 0.04 respectively. The't'-value 1.712 as shown in the table above was found statistically insignificant (P>.05). But while comparing the mean values of both the groups, it has been observed that Haryana boxers have demonstrated better Agility than the Punjab boxers.

3.  The Mean and SD values of Punjab boxers on the sub-variable Balance as 26.70 and 6.03 respectively. However, Haryana boxers had Mean and SD values as 29.00 and 7.06 respectively. The Mean Difference and Standard Error Difference of Mean were 2.30 and 1.03 respectively. The't'-value 2.214 as shown in the table above was found statistically significant (P<.05). But while comparing the mean values of both the groups, it has been observed that Haryana boxers have demonstrated better Balance than the Punjab boxers.

4. The Mean and SD values of Punjab boxers on the sub-variable Coordination as 29.70 and 5.45 respectively. However, Haryana boxers had Mean and SD values as 29.12 and 6.06 respectively. The Mean Difference and Standard Error Difference of Mean were 0.57 and 0.91 respectively. The 't'-value 0.630 as shown in the table above was found statistically insignificant (P>.05). But while comparing the mean values of both the groups, it has been observed that Haryana boxers have demonstrated better Coordination than the Punjab boxers.

5. The Mean and SD values of Punjab boxers on the sub-variable Reaction Time as 0.22 and 0.01 respectively. However, Haryana boxers had Mean and SD values as 0.23 and 0.01 respectively. The Mean Difference and Standard Error Difference of Mean were 0.002 and 0.001 respectively. The 't'-value 1.227 as shown in the table above was found statistically insignificant (P>.05). But while comparing the mean values of both the groups, it has been observed that Punjab boxers have demonstrated better Reaction Time than the Haryana boxers.

6. The Mean and SD values of Punjab boxers on the sub-variable Power as 1.45 and 0.20 respectively. However, Haryana boxers had Mean and SD values as 1.31 and 0.13 respectively. The Mean Difference and Standard Error Difference of Mean were 0.14 and 0.027 respectively. The 't'-value 5.073 as shown in the table above was found statistically significant (P<.05). But while comparing the mean values of both the groups, it has been observed that Punjab boxers have demonstrated better Power than the Haryana boxers.

7. The Mean and SD values of Punjab boxers on the sub-variable Vital Capacity as 3.57 and 0.34 respectively. However, Haryana boxers had Mean and SD values as 3.69 and 0.32 respectively. The Mean Difference and Standard Error Difference of Mean were 0.11 and 0.053 respectively. The 't'-value 2.116 as shown in the table above was found statistically significant (P<.05). But while comparing the mean values of both the groups, it has been observed that Haryana boxers have demonstrated better Vital Capacity than the Punjab boxers.

8. The Mean and SD values of Punjab boxers on the sub-variable Resting Pulse Rate as 76.91 and 3.16 respectively. However, Haryana boxers had Mean and SD values as 74.32 and 2.84 respectively. The Mean Difference and Standard

Error Difference of Mean were 2.58 and 0.47 respectively. The 't'-value 5.440 as shown in the table above was found statistically significant (P<.05). But while comparing the mean values of both the groups, it has been observed that Haryana boxers have demonstrated better Resting Pulse Rate than the Punjab boxers.

9. The Mean and SD values of Punjab boxers on the sub-variable Peak Flow Rate as 363.66 and 94.84 respectively. However, Haryana boxers had Mean and SD values as 396.23 and 75.86 respectively. The Mean Difference and Standard Error Difference of Mean were 32.57 and 13.57 respectively. The 't'-value 2.399 as shown in the table above was found statistically significant (P<.05). But while comparing the mean values of both the groups, it has been observed that Haryana boxers have demonstrated better Peak Flow Rate than the Punjab boxers.

10. The Mean and SD values of Punjab boxers on the sub-variable Standing Height as 174.65 and 4.76 respectively. However, Haryana boxers had Mean and SD values as 172.67 and 5.66 respectively. The Mean Difference and Standard Error Difference of Mean were 1.97 and 0.82 respectively. The 't'-value 2.385 as shown in the table above was found statistically significant (P<.05). But while comparing the mean values of both the groups, it has been observed that Punjab boxers have demonstrated better Standing Height than the Haryana boxers.

11. The Mean and SD values of Punjab boxers on the sub-variable Body Weight as 71.65 and 3.10 respectively. However, Haryana boxers had Mean and SD values as 70.15 and 5.15 respectively. The Mean Difference and Standard Error Difference of Mean were 1.50 and 0.67 respectively. The 't'-value 2.230 as shown in the table above was found statistically significant (P<.05). But while comparing the mean values of both the groups, it has been observed that Haryana boxers have demonstrated better Body Weight than the Punjab boxers.

12. The Mean and SD values of Punjab boxers on the sub-variable Leg Length as 101.30 and 3.98 respectively. However, Haryana boxers had Mean and SD values as 100.30 and 5.07 respectively. The Mean Difference and Standard Error Difference of Mean were 1.00 and 0.72 respectively. The 't'-value 1.395 as shown in the table above was found statistically insignificant (P>.05). But

while comparing the mean values of both the groups, it has been observed that Punjab boxers have demonstrated better Leg Length than the Haryana boxers.

13. The Mean and SD values of Punjab boxers on the sub-variable Upper Leg Length as 50.76 and 2.22 respectively. However, Haryana boxers had Mean and SD values as 50.15 and 2.20 respectively. The Mean Difference and Standard Error Difference of Mean were 0.61 and 0.35 respectively. The't'-value 1.768 as shown in the table above was found statistically insignificant (P>.05). But while comparing the mean values of both the groups, it has been observed that Punjab boxers have demonstrated better Upper Leg Length than the Haryana boxers.

14. The Mean and SD values of Punjab boxers on the sub-variable Lower Leg Length as 50.55 and 1.98 respectively. However, Haryana boxers had Mean and SD values as 49.15 and 2.60 respectively. The Mean Difference and Standard Error Difference of Mean were 1.40 and 0.36 respectively. The't'-value 3.837 as shown in the table above was found statistically significant (P<.05). But while comparing the mean values of both the groups, it has been observed that Punjab boxers have demonstrated better Lower Leg Length than the Haryana boxers.

15. The Mean and SD values of Punjab boxers on the sub-variable Arm Length as 82.15 and 2.33 respectively. However, Haryana boxers had Mean and SD values as 80.76 and 3.20 respectively. The Mean Difference and Standard Error Difference of Mean were 1.38 and 0.44 respectively. The't'-value 3.127 as shown in the table above was found statistically significant (P<.05). But while comparing the mean values of both the groups, it has been observed that Punjab boxers have demonstrated better Arm Length than the Haryana boxers.

16. The Mean and SD values of Punjab boxers on the sub-variable Upper Arm Length as 36.14 and 1.26 respectively. However, Haryana boxers had Mean and SD values as 35.66 and 1.66 respectively. The Mean Difference and Standard Error Difference of Mean were 0.48 and 0.23 respectively. The't'-value 2.054 as shown in the table above was found statistically significant (P<.05). But while comparing the mean values of both the groups, it has been observed that Punjab boxers have demonstrated better Upper Arm Length than the Haryana boxers.

17. The Mean and SD values of Punjab boxers on the sub-variable Lower Arm Length as 46.59 and 2.93 respectively. However, Haryana boxers had Mean and SD values as 44.92 and 1.70 respectively. The Mean Difference and Standard Error Difference of Mean were 1.66 and 0.37 respectively. The't'-value 4.398 as shown in the table above was found statistically significant (P<.05). But while comparing the mean values of both the groups, it has been observed that Punjab boxers have demonstrated better Lower Arm Length than the Haryana boxers.

18. The Mean and SD values of Punjab boxers on the sub-variable Hip Width as 30.95 and 2.56 respectively. However, Haryana boxers had Mean and SD values as 31.00 and 2.16 respectively. The Mean Difference and Standard Error Difference of Mean were 0.050 and 0.37 respectively. The't'-value 0.133 as shown in the table above was found statistically insignificant (P>.05). But while comparing the mean values of both the groups, it has been observed that Haryana boxers have demonstrated better Hip Width than the Punjab boxers.

19. The Mean and SD values of Punjab boxers on the sub-variable Shoulder Width as 35.45 and 1.89 respectively. However, Haryana boxers had Mean and SD values as 34.96 and 1.34 respectively. The Mean Difference and Standard Error Difference of Mean were 0.48 and 0.25 respectively. The't'-value 1.881 as shown in the table above was found statistically insignificant (P>.05). But while comparing the mean values of both the groups, it has been observed that Punjab boxers have demonstrated better Shoulder Width than the Haryana boxers.

20. The Mean and SD values of Punjab boxers on the sub-variable Chest Width as 31.05 and 1.90 respectively. However, Haryana boxers had Mean and SD values as 30.22 and 2.03 respectively. The Mean Difference and Standard Error Difference of Mean were 0.82 and 0.31 respectively. The't'-value 2.650 as shown in the table above was found statistically insignificant (P>.05). But while comparing the mean values of both the groups, it has been observed that Punjab boxers have demonstrated better Chest Width than the Haryana boxers.

21. The Mean and SD values of Punjab boxers on the sub-variable Calf Girth as 38.71 and 1.76 respectively. However, Haryana boxers had Mean and SD values as 32.54 and 1.86 respectively. The Mean Difference and Standard

Error Difference of Mean were 6.17 and 0.28 respectively. The 't'-value 21.49 as shown in the table above was found statistically significant (P<.05). But while comparing the mean values of both the groups, it has been observed that Punjab boxers have demonstrated better Calf Girth than the Haryana boxers.

22. The Mean and SD values of Punjab boxers on the sub-variable Thigh Girth as 55.58 and 1.99 respectively. However, Haryana boxers had Mean and SD values as 51.51 and 2.73 respectively. The Mean Difference and Standard Error Difference of Mean were 4.07 and 0.37 respectively. The 't'-value 10.771 as shown in the table above was found statistically significant (P<.05). But while comparing the mean values of both the groups, it has been observed that Punjab boxers have demonstrated better Thigh Girth than the Haryana boxers.

23. The Mean and SD values of Punjab boxers on the sub-variable Chest Girth as 90.40 and 3.04 respectively. However, Haryana boxers had Mean and SD values as 88.95 and 4.16 respectively. The Mean Difference and Standard Error Difference of Mean were 1.45 and 0.57 respectively. The 't'-value 2.513 as shown in the table above was found statistically significant (P<.05). But while comparing the mean values of both the groups, it has been observed that Punjab boxers have demonstrated better Chest Girth than the Haryana boxers.

24. The Mean and SD values of Punjab boxers on the sub-variable Upper Arm Girth as 29.32 and 2.13 respectively. However, Haryana boxers had Mean and SD values as 25.92 and 1.13 respectively. The Mean Difference and Standard Error Difference of Mean were 3.39 and 0.27 respectively. The 't'-value 12.550 as shown in the table above was found statistically significant (P<.05). But while comparing the mean values of both the groups, it has been observed that Punjab boxers have demonstrated better Upper Arm Girth than the Haryana boxers.

25. The Mean and SD values of Punjab boxers on the sub-variable Lower Arm Girth as 25.86 and 1.20 respectively. However, Haryana boxers had Mean and SD values as 25.04 and 120 respectively. The Mean Difference and Standard Error Difference of Mean were 0.81 and 0.19 respectively. The 't'-value 4.286 as shown in the table above was found statistically significant (P<.05). But while comparing the mean values of both the groups, it has been observed that

Punjab boxers have demonstrated better Lower Arm Girth than the Haryana boxers.

## RECOMMENDATIONS OF THE STUDY

Although the investigator has put in his best efforts on the present study, still the topic has a wide scope for further research. Thus, for future research and in the light of the results and conclusions of the study, the following recommendations are made:

1. Physical education teachers and coaches may utilize the findings of the present study by preparing or modifying the existing training schedules for Punjab and Haryana Boxers.

2. The data regarding Physical, Physiological and Anthropometric Characteristics will help the coaches to adjust the training programme for elite Boxers.

3. Similar study may be under taken with other variable namely, biomedical and biomechanical in addition to the variables chosen in the present study.

4. A similar study may be undertaken with female individual sports and team sports as subjects.

5. It is recommended that the present study may be repeated by selecting subjects belonging to lower age groups.

# BIBLIOGRAPHY
## BOOKS

1. Garrett, Henry E. and Woodworth, R.S. (1981). Statistics in Psychology and Education. Vakils, Feffer and Simons Ltd., Bombay.

2. Phillips, Allon D and Hornak, James E, (1979). Measurement and Evaluation in Physical Education .John Wiley and Sons, New York.

3. Werner, W.K. Hoeger, Shoron, A. Hoeger, (1990). Physical Fitness, Fitness and Wellness, Englewood.

## JOURNALS AND PERIODICALS

1. Anna-Liisa Parm (2011), Relationships between anthropometric, body composition and bone mineral parameters in 7-8-year-old rhythmic gymnasts compared with controls, University of Tartu, Faculty of Exercise and Sport Sciences, Tartu, Estonia, Coll Antropol. 2011 Sep ;35 (3):739-45

2. Ann-Marie Knowles, Ailsa G. Niven. Mantha G. Fawkner and Joan M. Henretty (2008). A longitudinal examination of the influence of maturation on physical self-perceptions and the relationship with physical activity in early adolescent girls. Journal of Adolescence Volume 32, issue3, June 2009, 555-566.

3. Ahmed Nabieh Ibrahim Mohamed (2010). Anthropometric Measurements as a Significant for Choosing Juniors in Both Volleyball and Handball Sports. World Journal of Sport Sciences 3 (4): 277-289, 2010

4. Aman Singh Sisodiya, Monica Yadav. (2010).Relationship of Anthropometric Variables to Basketball Playing Ability. Journal of Advances in Developmental Research 1 (2) 2010: 191-194.

5. Carlos Fernando & Rita de (2012), Factors associated with physical inactivity in adolescents aged 10-14 years, enrolled in the public school network of the city of Salvador, Brazil, Rev. bras. epidemiol. vol.15 no 4.

6. Chandershekhar kapoot, kisan ravikiran, shettar S Svitha, (2010). Anthropometric and physiological profile of wrestlers, vol.33, no.2.

7. Charilaos Tsolakis & George Vagenas.(2010) Anthropometric, Physiological and Performance Characteristics of Elite and Sub-elite Fencers. Journal of Human Kinetics volume 23, January 2010, 89-95

8. Chandrasekhar kapoor, Kisan ravikiran, Shettar S.Savitha (2010). Anthropometric and physiological profile of wrestler. Journal of sports and sports science, vol 33, no-2, 16-22

9. Dan-Olof Rooth. (2010). Work out or out of work the labor market return to physical fitness and leisure sports activities. 26 November 2010.volume 18, issue 3, June 2011, 399-409.

10. Dr.Satbir Singh Sangha (2010). Comparison of physical fitness and personality traits among wrestlers across their level of participation, journal of sports and sports science, vol 33, No-4, 15-21.

11. Tania Abreu and Eliane Abreu (2010), Nutritional and anthropometric profile of adolescent volleyball athletes, Rev Bras Med Esporte vol.9 no.4 .

12. E.Ernst, T. Weihmayr, M. Schmid, M. Baumann and A. Matral. (2005). cardiovascular risk factors and hemorheology: physical fitness stress and obesity. 14th April 2005.volume 59, issue 3, March 1986, 263-269

13. Evdokia Varamenti and Theodoros Platanou. (2008).Comparison of Anthropometrical, Physiological and Technical Characteristics of Elite Senior and Junior Female Water Polo Players: A Pilot Study. *The Open Sports Medicine Journal*, 2008, *2*, 50-55.

14. Frank L. Smoll and Robert W. Schutz (2002) Physical fitness differences between athletes and non athletes: Do changes occur as a function of age and sex? Human Movement science, volume 4, issue 3, September 1985, 189-202.

15. Franck le Gall, Christopher Carling, Mark Williams and Thomas Reilly.(2008) Anthropometric and fitness characteristics of international, professional and amateur male graduate soccer players from an elite youth academy. 2 October 2008.volume 13, issu1, January 2010, 90-95

16. G.Vicente-Rodriguez, C. Dorado J. Perez-Gomez, J.J. Gonzalez-Henriquez and J.A.L. Calbet. (2004). Enhanced bone mass and physical fitness in young female handball players. Volume 35, issue 5, November 2004, 1208-1215.

17. G.Vicente-Rodriguez, J. Jimenez-Ramirez, I. Ara, J. A. Serrano-Sanchez, C. Dorado and J. A. L. Calbet.(2003). Enhanced bone mass and physical fitness in prepubescent footballers. 10 September 2003.volume 33, issue 5 November 2003, 853-859.

18. GIOVANI and PANTELIS THEODOROS NIKOLAIDIS (2012), Differences in Force-velocity Characteristics of Upper and Lower Limbs of Non-competitive Male Boxers, Nutrition and Dietics Department, Technical Educational Institute of Crete, GREECE; Laboratory of Human Performance and Rehabilitation, Department of Physical and Cultural Education, Hellenic Army Academy, GREECE.

19. GHORBANZADEH (2011) Determination of Taekwondo National Team Selection Criterions by Measuring Physical and Physiological Parameters, Scholars Research Library.

20. Gilenstam KM, Thorsen K, Henriksson-Larsén KB.(2011),Physical Correlates of skating Performance in Women's and men's ice hockey J Strength Cond Res. 2011 Aug;25(8):2133-42.

21. Guidetti L, Musulin A, Baldari C(2008), Physiological factors in middleweight boxing performance, University Institute of Motor Sciences, Rome, Italy, The Journal of sports medicine and physical fitness (impact factor: 0.85). 09/2008; 42(3):309-14.

22. Guidetti L, Musulin A and Baldari C(2002), Physiological factors in **middleweight boxing** performance,.Gulshan Lal Khanna and Indranil pubmed.gov Sep 2, 2002 Manna.(2006). Study of physiological profile of Indian boxer. 01 July 2006. 5, 90-98.

23. H. C. G. Kemper J. W. R. Twisk, W. van Mechelen, G. B. Post, J. C. Roos and P. Lips. A fifteen-year longitudinal study in young adults on the relation of physical activity and fitness with the development of the bone mass: the Amsterdam Growth and Health Longitudinal Study. Volume 27, issue 6, December 2000, 847.

24. Hencken, Clare and White, Colin (2006), Anthropometric assessment of Premiership soccer players in relation to playing position. European Journal of Sport Science, 6 (4). pp. 205-211.

25. Hoare DG. (2000). Predicting success in junior elite basketball players-the contribution of anthropometric and physiological attributes. J Sci Med Sport. 2000 Dec; 3(4):391-405.

26. Justin W.L. Keogh. (2011) Body Composition, Physical Fitness, Functional Performance, Quality of Life, and Fatigue Benefits of Exercise for Prostate Cancer Patients: A Systematic Review. Journal of Pain and Symptom Management.

27. Justin Keogh. (2006).The use of physical fitness scores and anthropometric data to predict selection in an elite under 18 Australian Rules football team. March 2006.volume, issues 1-2, May 2006, 143-150.

28. John S.Y. Chan, Alan C.N. Wong, Yu Liu, Jie Yu and Jin H. Yan. (2011). Fencing expertise and physical fitness enhance action inhibition.

29. Kaur R, Kaur A, Deepak, Singh J, and Singh S.(2001). Anthropometric and fitness profile of Asian Gold medalist male kabaddi players. Journal of sports and sports science NSNIS vol 17(3) 7-11

30. L.Suresh Roy, AK.Joy Singh, KH.Ranendra, K.Kosana Meitel, Ravi AK. (2010). Physical and Physiological Profiles of Elite Marathon Runners of Manipur. Journal of sports and sports science, vol 33, no-2, 23-29

31. M.S.Chouhan (2003).Correlation between selected anthropometric variables and middle distance running performance. Journal of sports and sports science. Vol 26, (3), 42-48

32. Martin A. Salah (2012) Anthropometric and Hemodynamic Profiles of Athletes and Their Relevance to Performance in the Mount Cameroon Race of Hope, Asian J Sports Med. 2012 June; 3(2): 99–104.

33. Monica G. Schick(2006), Physiological Profile of Mixed Martial Artists, Human Performance Laboratory, Department of Kinesiology, California State University, Fullerton, CA, USA.

34. M J Duncan, L Woodfield, and Y al-Nakeeb(2006), Anthropometric and physiological characteristics of junior elite volleyball players, Br J Sports Med. 2006 July; 40(7): 649–651.

35. Nail A. Clark Andrew M.Edwards R. Hugh Morton and Ronald J Butterly. (2008).Season to season variation of physiological fitness within a squad of professional male soccer players. Journal of Sports Science and Medicine (2008) 7, 157 – 165.

36. Percept Mot Skills. 2010. Relation of college students' self-perceived and measured health-related physical fitness. Aug; 111(1):229-39.

37. Pichini S, Ventura R, Palmi I, di Carlo S, Bacosi A, Langohr K, Abellan R, Pascual JA, Pacifici R, Segura J, Zuccaro P.(2010).Effect of physical fitness and endurance exercise on indirect biomarkers of growth hormone and insulin misuse:

Immunoassay-based measurement in urine samples.J Pharm Biomed Anal. 2010 Dec 1; 53(4):1003-10.

38. Paul S. Glazier, Giorgos P.Paradisis2 and Stephen-mark Cooper. (2000). Anthropometric and kinematics in uences on release speed in men's fast-medium bowling. Journal of Sports Sciences, 2000, 18, 1013± 1021.

39. Pui W. Kong and Hendrik de Heer. (2008).Anthropometric, gait and strength characteristics of Kenyan distance runners. Journal of Sports Science and Medicine (2008) 7, 499-504

40. P.Gopinath and Grace Hellina (2009). Correlation of selected anthropometric and physical fitness variable to handball performance. Vol 32, 25-48.

41. P. J. Maud (1983), Physiological and anthropometric parameters that describe a rugby union team, Br J Sports Med. 1983 March; 17(1): 16–23.

42. Richard J Simpson, Susan C Gray, Geraint D Florida-James (2009), Physiological variables and performance markers of serving soldiers from two "elite" units of the British Army. , J Sports Sci. 2009 Jun ;24 (6):597-604

43. Roopakala M. S, Anagha Suresh, Ashtalakshmi, Srinath, Ashok, Giridhar, Anand and Wilma Delphine Silva (2009). Anthropometric measurements as predictor of intraabdominal fat thickness. Indian J Physiol Pharmacol 2009; 53 (3): 259–264.

44. Rajdeep kaur, R.Mokha, V.Kharadkar and S.S.Kang, B.S.Tomar(2006). Positional defferenes in some anthropometric varables of senior national men basketball players. Vol 29, 23-37.

45. Rajesh Kumar Phor1 and H. S. Kang2 (2006) Comparison of Physical Fitness of Champion and Non-Champion Boxer at State Level .

46. Randy Zabukovec, Peter M. Tiidus (1995), Physiological and Anthropometric Profile of Elite Kickboxers, The Journal of Strength and Conditioning Research (impact factor: 1.83). 10/1995; 9(4).

47. Said El Ashker (2012) . Technical performance effectiveness subsequent to complex motor skills training in young boxers. European Journal of Sport Science 2012; Vol 12(6), 475-84.

48. Said El Ashker (2012) Effect of boxing exercises on physiological and biochemical responses of Egyptian elite boxers. Journal of Physical Education and Sport, Vol 12(1),111 - 116.

49. Said El Ashker (2011) Technical and tactical aspects that differentiate winning and losing performances in boxing International Journal of Performance Analysis in Sport, 356-364.

50. Santhiago V, Da Silva AS, Papoti M, Gobatto CA. (2011). Effects of 14-week swimming training program on the psychological, hormonal, and physiological parameters of elite women athletes. J Strength Cond Res. 2011 Mar; 25(3):825-32.

51. Shirley S.M. Fong and Gabriel Y.F.(2010). Does Taekwondo training improve physical fitness. 30 August 2010.volume 12, issue 2, May 2011, 100-106

52. Suresh Roy, A.K.Joy Singh, K.Kosana Meitel, L.Tiken Singh (2006). Physiological profile of national level fencers of India. Vol 29, 19-23.

53. Sidhu, J.S. (2009), Kinanthropometric Measurements in Players of Athletics and Boxing - A Comparative Study, Journal of Exercise Science and Physiotherapy, Vol. 5, No. 1: 56-61

54. Singh S, Nagarkoti NS and Hooda B S (2008). Anthropometric and physical fitness variables of 16 to 18 year old basketball players, journal of sports and sports science NSNIS vol 18 (4) 23-28

55. Simranjeet singh, N.S.Nagarkoti, B.S.Hooda (2008). A comparative study of anthropometric and physical fitness variables of 16 to 18 year old basketball players. Journal of sports and sports science vol 31, no 3, 31-36

56. Tim Gabbett, Jason Kelly and Troy Pezet (2007). A comparison of fitness and skill among playing positions in sub-elite rugby league players27 August 2007.volume 11, issue, November 2008, 585-592.

57. Br J Sports Med. 2000 August; 34(4): 303–307.

58. T. Gabbett (2000), Physiological and anthropometric characteristics of amateur rugby league players, Br J Sports Med. 2000 August; 34(4): 303–307.

59. Vishaw Gaurav, Mandeep Singh and Sukhdev Singh. (2010). Anthropometric characteristics, somatotyping and body composition of volleyball and basketball players. Vol. 1(3), pp. 28-32, December 2010.

60. Vishaw Gaurav, Mandeep Singh and Sukhdev Singh.(2011) A comparative study of somatic traits and body composition between volleyball players and controls. Indian Journal of Science and Technology. Vol. 4 No. 2 (Feb 2011).116-118

61. Vishaw Gaurav, Amandeep Singh and Sukhdev Singh (2011). Comparison of physical fitness variables between individual games and team games athletes. Indian Journal of Science and Technology. Vol. 4 No. 5 (May 2011).547-549

62. Warren B. Young and Luke Pryor (2006). Relationship between pre-season anthropometric and fitness measures and indicators of playing performance in elite junior Australian Rules football. 18 July 2006.volume 10, issue 2, April 2007, 110-118.

63. Wan Nudri WD[1], Ismail MN[2] and Zawiak H (2011) Anthropometric measurements and body composition of selected national athletes .

64. Wong P L. Chamari K, Dellal A, Wisløff U. (2009) Relationship between anthropometric and physiological characteristics in youth soccer players. Strength Cond Res. 2009 Jul; 23(4):1204-10

65. Yuhi Zhang (2010) An Investigation on the Anthropometry Profile and Its Relationship with Physical Performance of Elite Chinese Women Volleyball Players, Bachelor of Sport Science thesis, School of Health and Human Sciences Southern Cross University.

www.ingramcontent.com/pod-product-compliance
Lightning Source LLC
Chambersburg PA
CBHW060817050426

42449CB00008B/1692